LEARNING
FROM
ERROR

LEARNING FROM ERROR

Karl Popper's
Psychology of Learning

William Berkson
and
John Wettersten

Printed in the United States of America

OC788   10 9 8 7 6 5 4 3 2 1

ISBN 912050-74-8

Berkson, William
  Learning from error.

  Bibliography: p.
  1. Popper, Karl Raimund, Sir, 1902–   . 2. Learning,
Psychology of. 3. Education—Philosophy. I. Wettersten,
John. II. Title.
LB775.P632B47   1984   370.1   84-18881
ISBN 0-912050-74-8

CONTENTS

FOREWORD   IX

**PART I   POPPER ON THE PSYCHOLOGY
AND LOGIC OF DISCOVERY**

1. THE NOVELTY OF POPPER'S PSYCHOLOGY   3
The Root Problem   4
Popper's Theory of the Psychology of Discovery   6
Comparison with Selz's Theory of Trial and Error   8
Comparison with Gestalt Theory   10
Comparison with Piaget   12
Popper's Critique of Induction   13
Comparison with Stimulus-Response Psychology   17
Questions Raised by Popper's Theory   19

v

2. METHODOLOGY 23
The Demarcation Criterion 23
Popper's Theory of Scientific Method 26
Psychology and Psychologism 29
A Gap in Understanding Popper 33
Scientific Method and the Psychology of Discovery 35

**PART II CRITIQUE OF POPPER ON THE
CONNECTION BETWEEN THE PSYCHOLOGY
AND LOGIC OF DISCOVERY**

3. POPPER'S STANDARDS FOR SCIENCE 41
Inductivism 42
Conventionalism 44
Popper's Standards for Assessing Scientific Theories 47
The Rigidity of Popper's Theory of Standards 50
Popper on the Reliability of Beliefs 53
The Causes of Rigidity and the Conflict with Popper's
Psychology 60

4. POPPER'S ATTEMPT TO FREE METHODOLOGY
FROM PSYCHOLOGY 65
The Attempt in *The Logic of Scientific Discovery* 65
Later Discussion of Psychological Issues 72
Logic and Psychology 79

**PART III REASSESSING THE PROBLEM
SITUATION**

5. THE HISTORY OF THE INTERACTION BETWEEN
THE PSYCHOLOGY OF LEARNING AND THE
PHILOSOPHY OF SCIENCE 87
Bacon and the Method of Induction 88
Locke and the Psychology of Induction 89

CONTENTS

Hume and the Breakdown of the Logic of Induction 90
Kant: An Alternative to Associationism 92
Müller 94
Helmholtz 95
Wundt 101
Külpe 103
The Würzburg School 105
Selz 106
The Gestalt School 108
Bühler 112

6. FALLIBILISM VERSUS STIMULUS-RESPONSE
THEORY 117
The Reductionist Program in Psychology 117
Critique of the Reductionist Program 120
The Case of Tolman 124

7. THE CURRENT PROBLEM SITUATION 133
The Segregation of Psychology and Methodology 135
Three Associationist Blocks in Contemporary Psychology
and Philosophy 136
Current Views of the Problem Situation in the
Methodology of Science 141
A Reassessment of the Problem Situation
in Methodology 143

ACKNOWLEDGEMENTS 151

BIBLIOGRAPHY 153

FOREWORD:
THE PHILOSOPHY AND THE
PSYCHOLOGY OF LEARNING

The interface or the dividing area between the philosophy and the psychology of learning much deserves study. It is, to begin with, a most interesting and baffling place: where does the one field start and where does the other end? What assumptions does one field borrow from the other? It is also a very useful area, if only for the fact that a text belonging to one field may easily include material that obviously qualifies as belonging to the other. Now, some writers find this fact objectionable. Clearly, their objection—or, rather, the arguments in its favor—cannot but be a fusion of psychology and philosophy, and so objectionable by their very own lights. But even if not in the least objectionable, the fusion is admittedly problematic: we are better off when we are clear about the ingredients that go into our mixtures. Moreover, in this age of overspecialization, when few are well-versed in both philosophical and psychological literatures, we may well find that, unfortunately, the one accepts some assumptions on the authority of the other, and *vice versa*. Worse still, it is the same assumption which the two literatures so often borrow from each other on each other's authority!

The interface between learning theory in philosophy and learning theory in psychology is also a constant cause for annoyance. Clearly, the difference between the two is easily established. When we discuss the way a child learns to distinguish shapes and sizes, when we study the value of a *lingua franca* for the growth of knowledge, when we discuss incentives for learning, we are clearly not in the field of philosophy. What, then, is the concern of philosophy? Not *quid facti*, what is the fact of the matter, but *quid juris*, what is its status, is Immanuel Kant's celebrated answer. The status of real knowledge is absolute certainty, objectivity, indubitability, incorrigibility, unalterability— its being beyond all possible error. The statement concerns knowledge, however, not learning. How, then, are the two related here? Learning, perhaps one might say, is the act of the acquisition of knowledge. What process, however, and what stage of the process shall we deem learning? It would be easiest if we could agree that learning is the very last stage of the process of the acquisition of knowledge, the very grasp or comprehension of the fact that what the earlier parts of the process have furnished us with is, indeed, a proof. If we are forced to go further back and inquire about the earlier parts of the process, then we find ourselves in deep trouble. For the question, What constitutes proof proper in the various sciences? is highly controverted. Apriorists and aposteriorists disagree as to whether proof results from introspection or from inspection; nor is there agreement as to what exactly constitutes introspection or inspection. There is full agreement that we do learn, that somehow we do acquire knowledge by finding proof or at least some semblance of proof; but all else is contested. Of course, we could try to study the question, How do we learn? But to do so well, we have to learn properly; that is to say, follow the rules of learning as described in our best theory of learning. And so the dispute that should be settled by a learning study enters the very presuppositions of the same study!

This is not to concede that the two fields of study, the philosophy of learning and the psychology of learning, are one and the same. On the contrary, we may see their difference all the more clearly when we observe the way they interact, when we observe the influences that traverse their interface. When the associationist or orthodox associationist, philosophical theory of knowledge as empirical generalization from observations was entrenched, a parallel associationist or orthodox associationist psychological theory of knowledge as the outcome of acts of association of perceived elements was also entrenched. Indeed, both were established on the authority of John Locke and of his friend Sir Isaac Newton. When David Hume later questioned philosophical associationism—he said generalizations are never proofs, since when we generalize we plainly jump to conclusions—he did not question psychological associationism. He did not question the fact, but only its status. He took for granted that associationism was an observed fact. In this he was clearly in error: he plainly jumped to conclusions here, and by his own lights!

Associationism put down very strong roots. It is still widely popular, after nearly two centuries of empirical refutations of it. It keeps alive by hiding in philosophy when attacked in psychology, and *vice versa*. It is therefore worthwhile to present its history, its philosophical and psychological variants, and their refutations. Whether we accept the refutations as conclusive, or examine them, or seek new unrefuted variants of them, is another matter.

The great merit of the early work of Sir Karl Popper, published only half a century or so later, is that it declares the field open and discusses the different options. We can deny that there is a parallel between learning theory in philosophy and in psychology. We can then declare associationism true in the one and false in the other, or *vice versa.* Or we can assert the parallelism and declare associationism true in both or false in both. Though there are, in the history of the situation, examples of thinkers who have opted for each of the alternatives just mentioned, there is hardly any discussion of the overall situation, and even Popper overlooked his own study of the matter.

In their thrilling *Learning from Error: Popper's Psychology of Learning,* Berkson and Wettersten tell the story of the situation and claim that it is easier to comprehend Popper's philosophy of learning in conjunction with his psychology of learning. They criticize his presentation of the one as independent of the other. Their criticism is not only historical, from the fact that traditionally and to the present the interface of the two fields sees much traffic in ideas: they also criticize Popper's very rationale for the separation which he has affected. Early in his classical *magnum opus, Logik der Forschung,* Popper calls for the separation between the two fields with an unanswerable argument: if the philosophy of science is based on psychology, and if psychology, as a science, is based on the philosophy of science, then clearly we have two questionable theories validating each other, which is highly question-begging! This argument is, I repeat, unanswerable, but it is directed only against those who hold the view that science has the status of certainty or of some surrogate to it. This very idea, we remember, leads us to the idea of proof by inspection or by introspection. And with some exercise of elimination, we end up holding a variant of the philosophical theory which is the parallel of associationism in psychology. If we give up the idea of scientific proof to the extent of not even looking for any surrogate to certitude, if we fully admit that all science is, in Popper's idiom, conjectural knowledge, then clearly Popper's unanswerable argument ceases to hold against us—and this includes Popper himself, Berkson and Wettersten, as well as myself and many others—and we are free to present the two fields separately or in a fused fashion or both, depending on the task at hand. The liberalizing effect of this little volume is considerable. So is the challenge it offers to students of the two fields and their histories.

Joseph Agassi

Somerville, Massachusetts, December, 1983.

PART I

POPPER
ON THE PSYCHOLOGY
AND LOGIC
OF DISCOVERY

1
THE NOVELTY
OF POPPER'S PSYCHOLOGY

This book is a reassessment of the current problem situation in the fields of the psychology of learning and the philosophy of science. In particular, it is a reassessment of the contribution of Sir Karl Popper to both fields.

In the late nineteenth and early twentieth centuries, psychology and philosophy came to be regarded as quite distinct concerns: theories of scientific method and theories of the psychology of learning, especially, went their separate ways. In our view, this separation has made research in both fields more difficult. In fact the impetus for the development of both fields comes from common problems first considered in the nineteenth century. When the close connection of the two fields is understood, we believe that a new view of the problem situation in both fields is warranted. In particular, we see the work of Popper as of central importance for the psychology of learning, as well as for the understanding of scientific method.

THE ROOT PROBLEM

The problem common to both disciplines is, in a nutshell: If Immanuel Kant and David Hume are both wrong about the way the mind works, then how *do* we learn? According to Hume (1711–1776), the mind is a blank slate upon which sensations are written; all knowledge is derived from the association of these sensations. Kant (1724–1804), in contrast, believed that we have an *inborn framework* which we *use actively* in absorbing sensation. Learning is the result of the accumulation of experience from this process, as well as of the association of ideas which we have experienced. It is also possible to discover the inborn framework by analysis.

There was some confirmation of Kant's view during the first part of the nineteenth century. In Germany, Johannes Müller (1801–1858) showed that optic nerves, and only optic nerves, cause visual sensation. He took this to confirm the existence of an inborn structure which receives sensation. The mind, therefore, could not be the blank slate Hume had visualized. However, Hermann Helmholtz (1821–1894) showed that although experience is interpreted through a framework, the framework is at least partially *learned*. Memory influences perception, just as it obviously influences the understanding of language. So Kant could not be correct in believing that the framework we use to interpret sensation is entirely independent of experience.

The lesson of this history seems to be that learning must involve some kind of interplay of inborn capacities and experience—but what kind of interaction? and exactly

4

how does the interplay take place? In wrestling with this underlying problem, the tendency of thinkers in the psychology of learning and the methodology of science has been to return, sometimes unwillingly, to the positions of either Hume or Kant. Too often the result has been a misdirection of effort, with attempts to confirm positions already refuted and with a slighting of some fundamental issues.

One cause of the failure to overcome the Kant/Hume dichotomy is *the assumption that the learning process gives us the truth.* Although some allowance for the possibility of error has had to be made, the learning process has been viewed basically as a process of acquiring knowledge possessing *certainty.* A central problem resulting from this assumption has been to find the source of certainty. Hume had put the source in sensation, Kant in our inborn framework. Later thinkers, making the same assumption of certainty, have been pushed into one or the other untenable position.

This assumption of certainty is linked to a second; namely, that science is fully true. John Locke (1632–1704) viewed sensation as the source of certainty, and was concerned to provide a description of the mental processes which can lead us to scientific knowledge. He and then Hume had the contemporary example of Isaac Newton before them. Kant had a similar aim—to show how the certain knowledge exemplified by Newton's theory was possible. As long as it was presumed that science is fully true, the psychology of learning would need a description of the theory which could lead to such certainty.

In order to resolve the dichotomy, it is necessary to reject the presumption of fully reliable knowledge in either the philosophy of science or the psychology of learning. That breakthrough has been made by Popper. He has asserted that some part of our learning—both personal and scientific—involves *rejection* of what we formerly took to be true, and he has developed theories of the psychology

5

of learning and the methodology of science which are based on this insight. When the signficance of his ideas is understood, the current scene in learning theory and in the philosophy of science appears in a new light.

POPPER'S THEORY OF THE PSYCHOLOGY OF DISCOVERY

Sir Karl Popper is well-known for his ideas on scientific method. But it has also been recognized recently that some of his ideas belong to the field of psychology.[1] In particular, his theory of the growth of knowledge belongs to the tradition in psychology which regards learning not as a passive reception of information, but rather as the result of *active attempts to solve problems by trial and error.* What has not been recognized, even by Popper himself, is that his theory of trial and error is a distinct departure from other trial and error theories of thinking and learning.

We may grasp the essentials of any theory of trial and error by seeing how it characterizes a *problem.* For Popper, an important kind of problem is *the experience of something contrary to our expectations.* The upsetting or dis-

1. See Donald T. Campbell, "Evolutionary Epistemology", in *The Philosophy of Karl Popper,* ed. Paul Arthur Schilpp, pp. 413–463. Campbell does not note the distinctive character of Popper's theory of trial and error, which is our subject here. W.W. Bartley, in his "Theory of Language and Philosophy of Science as Instruments of Educational Reform: Wittgenstein and Popper as Austrian Schoolteachers", in *Methodological and Historical Essays in the Natural and Social Sciences,* ed. Robert S. Cohen and Marx W. Wartofsky, pp. 307–337, notes that Popper's ideas have their roots in early twentieth century German psychology. However, he erroneously asserts that Popper's ideas do not appear novel against this background. Joseph Agassi explains the novelty of Popper's philosophy of science, especially in relation to Whewell, in his "The Novelty of Popper's Philosophy of Science", *International Philosophical Quarterly,* 8 (1968):422–463 (reprinted in Agassi's *Science in Flux*). While we are not in full agreement with Agassi's characterization of the relation of Popper's views to past views, our central point in this chapter parallels—for psychology—the point Agassi makes concerning Popper's philosophy.

appointing of our expectations initiates the process of trial and error. The trials are attempts to correct our expectations so that they are consistent with the surprising event. An error in the attempt is indicated by a failure to account for both the surprising event and our other past experiences. Even a revision of our views which passes this test may, of course, be shown wrong by additional experiences which upset the new expectations.

In his essay "The Bucket and the Searchlight: Two Theories of Knowledge," Popper explains his conception in more detail, through his idea of the 'horizon of expectations':

> At every instant of our pre-scientific or scientific development we are living in the centre of what I usually call a 'horizon of expectations'. By this I mean the sum total of our expectations, whether these are subconscious or conscious, or perhaps even explicitly stated in some language. Animals and babies have also their various and different horizons of expectations though no doubt on a lower level of consciousness than, say, a scientist whose horizon of expectations consists to a considerable extent of linguistically formulated theories or hypotheses.
>
> The various horizons of expectations differ, of course, not only in their being more or less conscious, but also in their content. Yet in all these cases the horizon of expectations plays the part of a frame of reference: only their setting in the frame confers meaning or significance on our experiences, actions, and observations.
>
> Observations, more especially, have a very peculiar function within this frame. They can, under certain circumstances, destroy even the frame itself, if they clash with certain of the expectations. In such a case they can have an effect upon our horizon of expectations like a bombshell. This bombshell may force us to reconstruct, or rebuild, our whole horizon of expectations; that is to say, we may have to correct our expectations and fit them together again into something

like a consistent whole. We can say that in this way our horizon of expectations is raised to and reconstructed on a higher level, and that we reach in this way a new stage in the evolution of our experience; a stage in which those expectations which have not been hit by the bomb are somehow incorporated into the horizon, while those parts of the horizon which have suffered damage are repaired and rebuilt. This has to be done in such a manner that the damaging observations are no longer felt as disruptive, but are integrated with the rest of our expectations. If we succeed in this rebuilding, then we shall have created what is usually known as an *explanation* of those observed events [which created the disruption, the problem].[2]

Popper has also characterized the trial and error process in *logical* terms: a problem is a *contradiction* between a *universal statement* describing the expectation and a *singular statement* describing the conflicting experience. A trial is the positing of a new universal statement from which—if the trial is successful—can be deduced both the formerly conflicting statement and other singular statements describing past experiences. However we describe the process—and there are difficulties here, as we shall see—Popper believes that it is a pervasive aspect of our thinking and learning. He says, "The process of learning consists largely in such corrections [of our expectations that have been upset]."[3]

COMPARISON WITH SELZ'S THEORY OF TRIAL AND ERROR

The distinctive nature of Popper's view of trial and error may be seen by comparison with the views of Otto Selz

2. Karl Popper, *Objective Knowledge*, p. 345.
3. Popper, *Objective Knowledge*, p. 344.

(1881–1943), whose work just preceded Popper's in the 1920's and whose views form the basis of contemporary efforts to simulate human problem solving in electronic computers—that is, to create 'artificial intelligence'.

For Selz, a problem is essentially a gap in our knowledge, and the process of trial and error is an attempt to fill the gap correctly. To use Selz's terminology, all problem solving is an attempt to complete a 'complex' which has a gap in it. The critical feature of these complexes is that they have *logical* structure.[4]

A typical Selzian problem is something like this: a subject is asked: "Name the teacher of the following person: Plato." According to Selz, the task (name the teacher) combines with the specific name (Plato) to set up in the subject's mind an incomplete complex of the form 'x R Plato?', where 'x R y' means that x was the teacher of y, and the question mark indicates the task of finding out what x, the gap, is. The subject would then search his memory to find the solution, "Socrates." Selz calls this kind of problem solving, which draws on knowledge already acquired, 'reproductive thinking'. In 'productive thinking', the completed complex would not already exist in the memory, and there would be a trial and error attempt to find an element that would complete the complex successfully.

Though we have described only a few of Selz's basic ideas, we can see already how much Popper's theory departs from them. First, the two men differ on the nature of problems. Selz takes a problem to be an incomplete structure, whereas Popper regards it as a conflict between an

---

4. Otto Selz, *Über die Gesetze des geordneten Denkverlaufs* and *Zur Psychologie des Produktiven Denkens und des Irrtums*. For accounts of Selz's work in English, see the excellent historical survey by George Humphrey, *Thinking*, Chap. 5; and see the translation of Selz's own summary article in George Mandler and Jean Matter Mandler, *Thinking*. The debt of 'artificial intelligence' approaches to Selz's work is explained in Allen Newell and Herbert A. Simon, *Human Problem Solving*.

already complete theory or expectation and a newly observed fact. Secondly, the nature of the trials is different. Selzian trials are attempts to *complete* a structure, and Popperian trials are attempts to *change* it. Again, the two hold contrasting views of old and new knowledge. Selz sees the new knowledge resulting from (productive) problem solving as an *extension* of old knowledge in a direction already determined by the old structure. Popper believes that the new knowledge involves *correction* of the old.

To use an analogy, Selz's process of problem solving is like a search for the piece which fills a gap in a jigsaw puzzle. Popper's approach can be likened to that of a painter who discovers, while finishing a landscape, that he has omitted an element essential to the effect he is striving toward. He has not only to paint in the missing element, but to retouch or even completely repaint the picture.

These comparisons show that though Popper's and Selz's views are different, they may also be complementary. For further insight into Popper's ideas, let us compare them with those which they most resemble—the theories of the Gestalt school and of Jean Piaget—and with those which they oppose most deeply—the stimulus-response theories.

COMPARISON WITH GESTALT THEORY

The Gestalt theorists view a problem as a difficulty in achieving a goal.[5] A paradigm of such a problem is the case of a toddler shown a cake on a low table; when he rushes toward the cake, he finds his way blocked by a three-sided

5. For a survey of the Gestalt theories of problem solving, see Humphrey, *Thinking*, Chap. 4.

enclosure. The child surveys the situation and discovers a solution: with sudden insight, he turns with a cry of delight and runs around the enclosure to eat the cake.

In this case, the process of insight is supposed to involve a 'recentering' of the Gestalt. Instead of the Gestalt being "cake/barrier", it is now "cake/barrier with path around it". The idea of recentering resembles Popper's theory in that learning consists not only of the accumulation of information, but of a change in our views. However, the nature of that change is different in Gestalt theory. As in the case of Selz, the new knowledge—in this case the new Gestalt—does not involve a *rejection* of past beliefs.

There is also a significant difference in the conception of a problem. Though the Gestalt theorists see a problem as a kind of tension, it is a tension caused by a blocked effort to achieve a goal. For Popper, the tension is a conflict between incompatible views of the world. One might assimilate the views of Popper and Gestalt theory to each other by saying that Popper points out one kind of block to one kind of goal: the goal being a coherent horizon of expectations, and the block a conflict between new experience and old expectations. The views are probably compatible in this sense, but the Gestalt theorists do not recognize the kind of problem which Popper has felt is central to learning.

Finally, Popper has never shared the Gestalt ideology preached by Max Wertheimer (1880–1943), Wolfgang Köhler (1887–1967), and Kurt Koffka (1886–1941). In their view, all perception and learning involves Gestalts, and these wholes cannot be analyzed fruitfully in terms of their parts and the relations among the parts. Only laws expressing relations between wholes are permissible. It was this "structural monism"[6] which separated the Ges-

6. This characterization of the Gestalt view was made by Egon Brunswik, also a student of Bühler. See G.W. Hartmann, *Gestalt Psychology*, p. 284.

talt *school* from the other followers of Oswald Külpe (1862–1915), including Selz and Popper's teacher, Karl Bühler (1879–1963). Like Bühler, Popper feels that 'Gestalten' are real enough but are not the whole story. He believes that they are only one kind of hypothesis the mind can make in interpreting and explaining experience, and that investigation of the *logical* relations between different hypotheses and experiences can profitably be examined.

COMPARISON WITH PIAGET

Like Jean Piaget (1896–1980), Popper has been fundamentally concerned with cognitive growth and change. But despite the similarity of concern, the two seem to be describing different worlds. Perhaps the most basic difference lies in Popper's view of the dominant influence of the search for a coherent and complete horizon of expectations. He believes we have a kind of *cognitive hunger*, a need for knowledge of what can be expected from the world.

Piaget, in contrast, seems mainly concerned with the development of cognitive *skills*.[7] He argues that our greatest need is to master the world, to be able to manipulate it to our own advantage. What he tries to describe is the development of the mental skills we need in order to act. In the first stages, these are skills in carrying out actual physical operations; in the higher stages, new mental operations are involved. He is concerned primarily with the growth of *intelligence*, whereas Popper is concerned mainly with

7. For a general survey of Piaget's views, see John H. Flavell, *The Developmental Psychology of Jean Piaget*; and specifically on the relation between older and newer mental frameworks, see pp. 239–240; as well as Jean Piaget, "Development and Learning", *Journal of Research in Science Teaching*, vol. 2, especially p. 184, and his "The Role of the Concept of Equilibrium in Psychological Explication", *Six Psychological Studies*, ed. by D. Elkind, pp. 100–113.

the growth of *knowledge* in both the individual and mankind.

The differences in concern seem to have led to views that are at points in conflict. Piaget believes that intellectual development is accompanied by rejection of some false view, i.e. that a taller glass of water can always contain more liquid. But such rejections are, so to speak, byproducts of our efforts to develop our skills—skills which improve primarily as a result of maturation and of our need to master the world. Specific experiences, and in particular the refutation of beliefs, are not the engines of progress. Nor do the higher level skills involve rejection of the lower: skills cannot be refuted, but can only fall into disuse. Indeed, Piaget holds that the lower level skills are in fact incorporated into the higher.

How Popper's views might be tested against those of Piaget is an interesting question to which we shall later turn.

POPPER'S CRITIQUE OF INDUCTION

Since Popper's rejection of the stimulus-response approach to psychology is based on his critique of Hume, let us begin by examining that critique.

Popper first formulated his theories while working with underprivileged children in the aftermath of World War I. This was, of course, a time of great social disruption, when the horizon of expectations of all Europe had been shattered by the war.[8] Popper believed that the need for a secure framework of expectations was an important moti-

8. The events referred to here are described by Popper in his autobiography in *The Philosophy of Karl Popper*, ed. P.A. Schilpp; published separately as *The Unended Quest*. Popper has indicated to one of us (Berkson) in a private communication that the sequence of development of his ideas was as noted in our text.

vation in the lives of the children he worked with, and indeed in himself.

He soon realized that his theory of the repeated formation and disruption of a system of expectations was in conflict with Hume's theory of the formation of our expectations. Hume's argument is that our notion of cause and our expectations about the future arise from the repeated experience of conjoined events. One event occurs, and another follows immediately in the same or a neighboring place. With the repetition of such experiences, the occurrence of one will give rise to an expectation of the other. Popper, following Kant, viewed these expectations as expressions of universal theories, and so interpreted Hume as proposing that the knowledge of universal laws arises from particular experiences.

Popper developed a powerful argument against Hume's theory, based on his own view of learning. He argued that the repetition of particular events could not be the sole psychological basis for the learning of universal theories. Popper pointed out that as a matter of fact there are no exact repetitions of events, and that as a matter of logic, *any* event may be regarded as an imperfect repetition of another. The logical principle he had in mind was Bertrand Russell's principle of abstraction.[9] According to this principle, any group of individuals may be regarded as constituting a class. Each member of the class resembles each other in that it is a member of that class. Thus we see that on the one hand, repetition is never perfect; and that on the other, anything can be regarded logically as an imperfect repetition of any other thing. Any systematic selec-

9. Karl Popper, *Conjectures and Refutations*, pp. 44–45. Popper refers to his argument as a "purely logical" one, though he does not mention the principle of logic involved: that information was given to one of us (Berkson) in a private communication. When we apply it to the argument in *Conjectures and Refutations*, we see that the argument is not in fact *purely* logical, as there are also empirical assumptions involved. The argument in our text, then, is an expanded and somewhat revised version.

tion of some events as repetitions must therefore be based on a *preconceived* point of view, one which cannot itself be derived from repetition of particular events.

Popper contended that the necessity of a preconceived point of view made Hume's theory (of the "primacy of repetitions" of singular events[10]) untenable. Furthermore, this preconceived point of view has an element of universality in it, in that it goes beyond previous experience. Therefore, there can be no such thing as a pure 'induction' from specific sensations to general ideas. This criticism of psychological induction, we should note, does not exclude all kinds of generalization. For example, someone arriving in England and seeing five people carrying umbrellas might think: "perhaps all Englishmen carry umbrellas." Popper's critique does not exclude such thinking. However, for the pure inductivist the general concepts of 'umbrella' and 'Englishman' would themselves have to have been derived by generalization from experiences free from the taint of interpretation by general ideas. It is this derivation that Popper rejects.

Popper's critique of induction brings to light some of the other important features of his view of the nature of human thought. For one thing, he rejects the doctrine that all knowledge is derived from sensation. In this, he was following the dominant trend in psychology in the German-speaking world. What distinguished Popper's rejection was his realization that if no conscious experience is 'pure'—that is, free from interpretation—then the whole subject of learning from experience needed a deep change, and facile presumptions about 'generalization', 'abstraction', and 'induction' had to be re-examined. In particular, Popper felt that new general conceptions are developed partly from the conflict between more general ideas and more particular new experiences. The different levels of

10. Karl Popper, *The Logic of Scientific Discovery*, p. 422.

generality are implicated in the problem which stimulates and guides the search for new ideas, and so influences the construction of the new general theories or expectations.

A second feature of Popper's view of the nature of thinking is his concept of the mind as being relentlessly active in its attempts to understand the world.[11] An active view of the mind was also held by the Würzburg school, to which Selz belonged, and by the more modern followers of Selz, who have designed computer simulations of human problem solving. However, the degree of activity posited by Popper is more extreme than that proposed by the Selzians: it involves a constant testing of our most fundamental assumptions about the world, not just testing of attempts to *extend* our knowledge. For Popper, the acts of perception and thinking are like attempts to understand a difficult text: we read one part, guess as to its meaning, look to another part, see if that is consistent, or guess where our interpretation needs change, and so on. This activity is something we indulge in not occasionally, but rather constantly. We have been born with the task of developing a realistic set of expectations about the world based on the coded messages we receive from it. We can't even be sure of the code but must keep checking on it. For example, Popper thinks that the periodic reversal in our impression of the optical illusion of the Necker cube is a result of trying out one interpretation, proving it wrong, trying another, and so on.[12]

In sum, it is evident that Popper's view is practically a negation of Hume's. Hume depicts the mind as a passive receiver of pure, discrete impressions which it stores and with repetition automatically generalizes. According to

11. Karl Popper, *The Open Society and Its Enemies*, p. 260, and the essay "The Bucket and the Searchlight", *Objective Knowledge*, pp. 341–61.
12. Popper explained his ideas on the Necker cube in a response to comments on Karl Popper and John C. Eccles, *The Self and Its Brain* at the 1978 meeting of the Eastern Division of the American Philosophical Association.

Popper, the mind actively seeks and attempts to understand experience, which comes to the individual's consciousness in an already interpreted form involving many different levels of generality: we seek to improve these generalizations by imaginatively changing and adjusting them to resolve conflicts in our understanding of our experience.

COMPARISON WITH STIMULUS-RESPONSE PSYCHOLOGY

The stimulus-response and the associationist theories of learning are in essence an external and internal version of the same theory.[13] Instead of claiming that all learning is an association of ideas, the stimulus-response school claims that all learning is an association of stimuli and of stimuli with responses. Hume argues that the association of ideas is the result of repetition under certain conditions; the stimulus response school contends that the association of stimuli and responses is the result of the same.

Because of this basic similarity of viewpoint, Popper's criticism of psychological induction applies with equal force to the stimulus-response approach. The association of stimuli and responses cannot only be due to repetition of objective stimuli. A stimulus will always be a stimulus *as interpreted by the individual*, and a repetition will be a repetition *from the viewpoint of the individual*. According to Popper's argument, that viewpoint cannot itself be

13. See Gardner Murphy, *Historical Introduction to Modern Psychology*. For a critique of the stimulus-response view from a Popperian viewpoint, see "Autobiography of Karl Popper", *The Philosophy of Karl Popper*, ed. Paul Arthur Schilpp, pp. 38, 61; R. James, "Conditioning is a Myth", *World Medicine*, 18 May 18 1977, pp. 25–28; John Wettersten, "Methods in Psychology: a Critical Case Study of Pavlov", *Philosophy of the Social Sciences*, 4 (1974):17–34; and John Wettersten, "Toward a Scientific Psychology. A Popperian Approach," Ph.D. dissertation, Boston University, 1970.

17

derived from the repetition of events. Therefore, the attempt to make the repetition of stimuli and responses the sole basis of learning collapses.

Incidentally, Popper's critique also undercuts the 'behaviorist' epistemology which has so often been associated with the stimulus-response approach. Since there is an element of personal judgment in the interpretation of what a stimulus is, there is room for variation and error from person to person, including the scientist-observer. This means that the element of *conjecture* and the possibility of error is unavoidable in psychological research—and it seems that the attempt to avoid conjecture is a basic motive of the behaviorist, stimulus-response approach.

One of the most telling criticisms of the stimulus-response approach regards the nature of goals. Stimulus-response psychology takes *needs* as fundamental, since one can imagine them as mere aches when they are unsatisfied; we need not ascribe any cognitive content to a need. *Goals,* on the other hand, do have cognitive content, and involve our ideas about what might happen in the future. If Popper's critique of psychological induction is correct, then the repeated fulfillment of a need cannot by itself create a goal (seeking what fulfilled the need), for the interpretation of an event as a repetition is something which cannot be derived from single stimuli or responses alone. Therefore, E.C. Tolman's hope of reducing goals to a stimulus-response complex cannot be fulfilled.[14]

Once we reject the possibility of explaining goals as a stimulus-response complex, we also reject the possibility of a successful stimulus-response theory of problem solving. A problem is some kind of difficulty in achieving a goal, and the search process involved in coming to a solution is guided by a person's conception of the goal and of the difficulty. Therefore the active searching and probing

14. John Wettersten, Ph.D. dissertation, p. 197 ff., and this book, Chap. 6.

which is for Popper and Selz the essence of mental activity cannot be reduced to the passive storing of certain stimuli and responses in a certain order.

This rejection of the stimulus-response program, we should note, does not imply that reward and punishment have no effect on people. Nor does it exclude the possibility that the way events are repeated and associated has a profound effect on our beliefs. What it does mean is that the life of the mind and the actions which spring from it cannot be reduced to an association of external events.

QUESTIONS RAISED BY POPPER'S THEORY

Popper's theory, considered as empirical psychology, raises a number of intriguing questions. First, what is the *scope* of Popper's theory? That is, when do we learn by the kind of conjectures and refutations that Popper describes, and when do we learn by other methods? The kind of learning that takes place in school when we study, say, the Pythagorean theorem, evidently is different from the process that the originator of the theorem went through. Though trial and error likely influence our understanding of what we are taught, the information we receive also plays a role, and the problem of understanding what we are taught is different from one of upset expectations. In the direct and explicit communication of information, what role does Popper's kind of trial and error play, if it plays any at all?

Further, when does Popper's kind of trial and error apply, and when do we learn instead by the gap-filling process described by Selz and the artificial intelligence school? If Popper is correct that fundamental revision of our views is an important aspect of our thinking, it would pose a challenge to the artificial school to create programs not only to simulate the exploration of a 'problem space', but also to simulate the *reformulation* of these problem spaces.[15]

Another issue concerns Popper's description of our expectations in terms of universal statements, our experiences in terms of singular statements, and the upsetting of an expectation in terms of a contradiction between such statements. Is this logical terminology an apt description of what happens psychologically? If an expectation has not been formulated in language, then (following Popper's view of logic) an upset expectation is not, strictly speaking, a contradiction. When do we see an experience as conforming to our expectations, and when do we see it as conflicting? In other words, what is the psychological correlate of the contradiction Popper describes?

A third set of questions concerns psychological induction. If the formation of our more general ideas is influenced by our previous more general ideas, more specific experiences, and the logical relations between these, what is the nature of the influence? If there is no pure psychological induction, is there an impure variety? How do expectation and experience interact in leading to new expectations?

Another question, which has been noted by Popper himself, concerns the effect of emotions on our willingness to reconsider our previous beliefs.[16] When do we tend to turn a blind eye to refuting evidence, and when do we pursue it?

A fifth set of questions bears upon the relation between Popper's and Piaget's views of child development. One interesting problem is the nature of the interaction of beliefs and expectations with skills in thinking. According to Pi-

---

15. For the notion of 'problem space', see Newell and Simon, *Human Problem Solving.*
16. Popper, *Conjectures and Refutations*, p. 49. Y. Fried and Joseph Agassi have taken up the idea that neurosis is a kind of dogmatism, but have claimed that it properly characterizes psychosis rather than neurosis. See their *Paranoia.*

aget, the 'structures' of the skills at higher stages are expansions without conflict of the structures at lower levels. The development from lower to higher stages is supposed to be mainly the result of maturation, and to take place in an invariable order. If Popper is correct about the importance of the need for a coherent horizon of expectations, we would expect experience, and in particular surprising experience, to play a greater role than allowed for by Piaget.

For example, we might expect the patterns of thinking at earlier stages to be tied to particular beliefs and expectations, and the *refutation* of these beliefs to accelerate the development from one stage to the next. A difference in rates of development in different cultures has already been observed; following Popper, one would expect the richer cultures to be those which offer quicker refutation of the child's mistaken views. Laboratory experiment might test whether development can be accelerated by the refutation of expectations, the suggestion of new ideas, and so on. Another variation which might be expected to evolve from Popper's view is a difference in pathways to development; we might find significantly different stages through which different individuals pass in arriving at higher stages. Again, this issue seems to be open to empirical examination.

What the investigation of these and other problems raised by Popper's theory will lead to, we cannot say. But whatever the eventual outcome, we can say this: the adoption of Popper's learning theory as a research program in psychology opens up many interesting avenues. The time is long overdue for the theory to come out of its background in Popper's philosophy and to cooperate and compete with the research programs of Gestalt psychology, stimulus-response psychology, Piaget, and the artificial intelligence school. We think it will prove a formidable competitor, and that we will all be benefactors of such a competition.

21

We have examined some of the distinctive features of Popper's theories on the psychology of thinking and learning, and some of the new questions they raise in psychology. Popper himself has not carried these ideas further within psychology; after spending a number of years in the 1920's studying psychology and developing his concepts, he switched his efforts to the methodology of science. However, these psychological theories were, as we shall show in the next chapter, a basis for his theories of scientific research.

2
METHODOLOGY

THE DEMARCATION CRITERION

At the same time that Popper was developing his ideas on the nature of creative thinking, he was also deeply concerned with what turned out to be a closely related problem—how to distinguish between true science and those systems of ideas that make false pretence to being scientific. This 'problem of demarcation', as Popper has called it, was more than an academic problem at the time—the early 1920s—that he was considering it. Karl Marx (1818–1883) and his followers had claimed scientific status for Marx's theories, and Marxists were using this claim to support their call for violence now to "shorten and lessen the birth pangs"[1] of the inevitable new social order.

As Popper has explained in his autobiography, he was at first attracted to Marxism and then horrified by its results, its pretences, and the irresponsibility of its advocates.[2] For Popper, therefore, the problem of demarcation had both personal and social implications. It also had significance within the human sciences, where Popper felt there was a mushiness from which physics was refreshingly free. He observed this mushiness particularly in the area of the psychology of the emotions, in which Sigmund Freud and Alfred Adler (with whom Popper had personal contact) were then pioneers.

The traditional view of the difference between true science and pseudoscience is that true science contains laws that are proven by observation and experiment, whereas pseudoscience contains merely fantasies unproven by fact. But it was clear to Popper that this traditional line of demarcation did not work. Even aside from his rejection of induction, Popper could see that the followers of Marx, Freud, and Adler could cite quantities of confirming evidence and apparently interpret every phenomenon in terms of the system they believed in. Moreover, Newton's theory of gravitation—which had been the paradigm of a scientific theory—had, it appeared, been recently (1919) refuted by Arthur Eddington's observations of a solar eclipse; and these observations supported Albert Einstein's new theory, which was inconsistent with Newton's.

Popper's new solution to the problem of demarcation was to define the difference between true science and pseudoscience as lying in the very *vulnerability to refutation* that had led to the downfall of Newton's gravitational theory. The ability of Freudians and Marxists to interpret

1. Popper discusses this passage of *Das Kapital* in *The Open Society and its Enemies*, vol ii, p. 86.
2. Karl Popper, *Unended Quest*, section 8.

every phenomenon in terms of their system revealed not the strength, but the weakness of the system, at least as it was understood by their followers. In explaining everything they explained nothing, for if one can account for both an event and its contrary in the same circumstances, then the theory has no true power of prediction or explanation.

Newton's and Einstein's theories, in contrast, clearly forbid some events from occurring. If these events do in fact occur, then the theories must be mistaken. For example, one of Newton's laws equates the total force on an object with the rate of change in its momentum. If there were a positive force on an object and no change in its momentum, then Newton's law would stand refuted.

Popper noted that this quality of 'testability' or 'falsifiability' is, first of all, a characteristic of the logical form of a theory. Statements of a universal form, such as "*All* electrical currents create a magnetic field about them," can be refuted by one event, whereas existential statements, such as "*There exists* a magic formula that calls up the devil," cannot be refuted by an observation, though they could conceivably be confirmed.

But Popper quickly perceived that the logical form of a statement was not sufficient for its testability to be sustained in practice, for it is always possible to adopt a policy which immunizes a theory against refutation. One can dismiss all reports of refuting evidence as false or malicious—a result of "repression" or "class prejudice"—or one can modify the theory *ad hoc*, such as by saying that it holds in all cases but the one just reported.

To capture the distinctive character of science, then, Popper saw that it was necessary not only to point out the logical form of a scientific theory, but also to characterize the rules or principles of method that the best scientists have adopted. These should include rejection of illegitimate ways of evading evidence that refutes a theory. But what exactly were these principles or rules of method?

25

It is at this point, we suspect, that Popper realized that the principles of method which could best support his demarcation criterion were the very principles that followed from his own theory of learning by trial and error.

POPPER'S THEORY OF SCIENTIFIC METHOD

Popper's ideas on scientific method are most easily understood by contrast to the methods following from inductive theories of learning. (His views on the special methods of the social sciences are not addressed in this book.) Two principles are basic to Popper's theory. First, research should not begin with an effort at unbiased observation, but rather with a focus on a *problem*. The researcher should ask: What is the problem? What are the alternative solutions? What are their strengths and weaknesses? Secondly, the effort to find a solution—or an improved solution—should not be a cautious effort to stick to the facts, but rather should combine *bold conjecture* with *severe criticism*.

Both principles follow from Popper's view of the nature of learning, and particularly of creative thinking. Because the mind always actively imposes an interpretation upon the data coming into it, there is no such thing as 'pure' observation untainted by theory, as is desired by some thinkers as a basis for induction. Objectivity comes not from being free of preconceptions, which is impossible, but rather from making our preconceptions explicit and critically comparing them to other theories. The mind is relentlessly problem-oriented, and articulating the problem and the problem situation is of great help. Such articulation makes the problem something we can discuss with others, study, and use as a guide to research and a stimulus to innovation. Subsequently, we can use the problem as a standard by which to judge the adequacy of the proposed solutions.

The second principle also follows from Popper's psychological theory. According to it theories cannot be induced from the facts; they can only be created by an imagination that leaps above particular instances in an effort to solve the problem and find a better general theory. But that creative leap can as easily be toward a mistaken theory as a correct one. To sort out the mistaken conjectures from the correct ones—in any case never a final and conclusive sorting—we must make a systematic effort at critically assessing the alternative theories.

To sum up, because we do in fact learn by conjectures and refutations in an effort to solve problems, the best way to make progress in the growth of knowledge is to focus on and articulate problems, to conjecture solutions boldly and imaginatively, and to assess the proposed solutions critically.

The importance of empirical testing follows from these basic principles. The aim of science is true explanation of the world of our experience, and scientific problems are inadequacies in our explanations of the results of observation and experiment. The strongest criticism of a theory purporting to explain the way things are is that it is contradicted by what we observe, or by the results of our experiments. Because of the importance of strong and systematic criticism of our conjectures, scientists should always strive to put their theories into a testable form. Further, when refutations occur, they should not be evaded by policies of dismissing contrary evidence, of making minimal *ad hoc* adjustments, or of surreptitiously changing the meaning of terms. These evasions only muddy the problem situation, hinder discovery of where we are mistaken, and so block progress toward better theories. Rather, after a critical assessment of the experimental report (often including repetition of the experiment), refuting evidence should be given full weight and in fact prized as a victory in the progress of science.

27

The idea that refutations are prized and central features of the development of science strongly supports Popper's idea that refutability separates true science from pseudo-science, and the rejection of *ad hoc* evasion of counter-evidence is precisely the principle of method needed to support testability as a working feature of science.

But in identifying the importance of refutation, Popper did more than recognize an existing practice of science. The dominance of the inductive view of scientific method has led many thinkers to regard refutation in a negative light, as a reflection of a personal shortcoming. This fear of refutation in turn puts a brake on the imagination in conjecturing new theories.

The power of Popper's methodology to stimulate progress in science positively is impressively illustrated by J.C. Eccles's account of the influence of Popper's ideas on the work in physiology for which Eccles won the Nobel Prize:

> Until 1945 I held the conventional ideas about scientific research. First, hypotheses grow out of the careful and methodical collection of experimental data, according to the inductive view of science deriving from Bacon and Mill. Even today many scientists believe in this method (though more recently a somewhat rigid and oversimplified form of Popper's ideas has begun to be fairly widely accepted). Secondly, I believed that the excellence of a scientist is judged by the reliability of his developed hypotheses, and by how much they stand firm as secure foundations for further advance. Thirdly, and this was for me perhaps the most important point: it is a sign of failure and in the highest degree regrettable if a scientist espouses an hypothesis which is falsified by new data and has to be scrapped.
>
> That was my trouble. I had long espoused an hypothesis which, I came to suspect, might have to be scrapped, and I was in a state of extreme depression about it. It was an hypothesis about synaptic trans-

mission between nerve cells, and I had become involved in a controversy in which I took up the theory that this transmission was largely electrical rather than due to a chemical transmitter substance (as held by Dale and Loewi). I admitted the presence of a slow, chemical component, but I believed that the fast transmission across the synapse was electrical.

It was at that time that I met Popper. Among the important things which I learned from him perhaps the most important was that it was not disgraceful to have one's own favourite hypotheses falsified. That was the best news I had had for a long time. I was persuaded by Popper, in fact, to formulate my electrical hypotheses of excitatory and inhibitory synaptic transmission with sufficient precision and rigour to invited strict experimental falsification; and that is what happened to them a few years later, very largely in a cooperative venture by my colleagues and myself, when in 1951 we started to do intracellular recording from motoneurones. Thanks to my tutelage by Popper I was able to work joyfully and devotedly in bringing about the death of a brain-child which I had nurtured for nearly two decades; and I was at once able to contribute to the theory of chemical transmission which was the brain-child of Dale and Loewi.

It was in this most personal manner that I had experienced the great liberating power of Popper's teachings on scientific method.[3]

PSYCHOLOGY AND PSYCHOLOGISM

We have explained how Popper's theory of good scientific method, including the demarcation principle, follows from his views on the nature of learning and creative thinking. However, this is not at all how Popper himself has pre-

3. John C. Eccles, "The World of Objective Knowledge", *The Philosophy of Karl Popper*, ed. by Paul Arthur Schilpp, pp. 349-350.

sented his ideas. In his first-published and classic work, *The Logic of Scientific Discovery*, Popper presented his methodological views as derived from the falsifiability principle, and stressed the need to uphold it as a principle of demarcation. Furthermore, he contended that theories of the psychology of discovery are irrelevant to methodology. In subsequent works he has explained his ideas on the psychology of discovery, but has continued to insist that his views on scientific method stand independent of his views of learning and generally that methodology should be quite independent of theories of the psychology of learning.

We believe that Popper's attempt to derive his methodology from the demarcation principle fails and that he is mistaken in his conviction that issues of the methodology of discovery can be strictly segregated from theories of the psychology of discovery. We believe as well that these mistakes have had harmful consequences for the understanding of Popper's psychology and methodology.

Popper's main argument in favor of segregating methodology from the psychology of learning is made in the section called "Elimination of Psychologism" in *The Logic of Scientific Discovery*. By 'psychologism' Popper means "the doctrine that statements can be justified not only by statements but also by perceptual experience."[4] As Popper notes, the effort to prove scientific knowledge purely on the basis of our immediate experience fails because statements can only be deduced from statements, not directly from experiences, and because induction does not prove anything. Furthermore, psychologism is part of a misguided subjectivist tradition in philosophy, one which tries to reduce the outside world of things to no more than a complex of our immediate experiences.

We agree with Popper that the elimination of psychologism, in this sense, is desirable. However, what Popper

4. Karl Popper, *The Logic of Scientific Discovery*, p. 94.

actually argues against in "Elimination of Psychologism" is not *psychologism*, but rather *psychology*. He says that

> the question how it happens that a new idea occurs to a man. . . may be of great interest to empirical psychology; but it is irrelevant to the logical analysis of scientific knowledge. This latter is concerned not with *questions of fact* (Kant's *quid facti?*) but only with questions of *justification or validity* (Kant's *quid juris?*) . . .I shall distinguish sharply between the process of conceiving a new idea, and the methods and results of examining it logically. As to the task of the logic of knowledge—in contradistinction to the psychology of knowledge—I shall proceed on the assumption that it consists solely in investigating the methods employed in those systematic tests to which every new idea must be subjected if it is to be seriously entertained.[5]

What Popper is discussing here is the irrelevance of psychological theory—theories of the mind's working—to his task, rather than psychologism as he has defined it. Given that the subtitle is misleading, is the argument still valid? Do the psychology and logic of discovery belong to separate realms, with theories of the mind irrelevant to the "logic" of discovery?

Admittedly, there is an important aspect of Popper's work which is not dependent on psychological theory. Popper pointed out that we can assess a scientific theory against experiments and observations whose results could potentially *contradict* the theory according to the rules of deductive logic. This idea of measuring progress by *testing* against the facts rather than by inductive proof from the facts was particularly important because it showed that we can measure the progress of science even when great theories, such as Newton's, are shown to be false. For

5. Ibid., p. 31.

31

those who held to the inductive view of method, such refutation threatened the 'bankruptcy of science', to use Poincaré's phrase.

However, Popper's logical analysis of testing is only one part of his theory of scientific method, contrary to what he implies in the above quotation. All of the points of method described in our previous section, including those which inspired Eccles, go beyond purely logical analysis; they are practical rules of method which can guide and inspire the researcher, both in theorizing and in testing. And in fact Popper explicitly recognizes that his rules of method—in particular the rule barring *ad hoc* modifications of a theory to avoid refutation—are not points of pure logic.

Popper characterizes his theory of method as follows:

> The theory of method, in so far as it goes beyond the purely logical analysis of the relations between scientific statements, is concerned with the *choice of methods*. . . . . Clearly [methodological] rules are very different from the rules usually called 'logical'. Although logic may perhaps set up criteria for deciding whether a statement is testable, it is not concerned with the question whether anyone exerts himself to test it. . . . Methodological rules are here regarded as *conventions*. They might be described as the rules of the game of empirical science. They differ from the rules of pure logic as do the rules of chess, which few would regard as part of *pure* logic . . . The result of an inquiry into the rules of the game of science—that is, of scientific discovery—may be entitled 'The Logic of Scientific Discovery'. . . . I shall try to establish the rules, or if you will the norms, by which the scientist is guided when he is engaged in research or in discovery, in the same sense here understood.[6]

According to Popper, we ultimately judge a system of

6. Ibid., pp. 49–54.

methodological rules by whether it "can be applied without giving rise to inconsistencies; whether it helps us; and whether we really need it."[7] But once we regard methodological rules as practical guidelines to be judged by their utility, then the laws of nature (including human nature) become relevant in assessing what is a better and what a worse method. The *'quid facti'* becomes relevant in judging the *'quid juris'*. For example, a rule that recommends a physically or psychologically impossible procedure is not a useful rule. In particular, recommending careful induction is not helpful if we cannot make "pure" observations and then inductions from these. And recommending a combination of bold conjectures and stringent criticism *will* be useful if we in fact do learn by conjectures and refutations.

In sum, the argument made by Popper in "Elimination of Psychologism" fails to show the irrelevance of the psychology of discovery to the logic of discovery. To base a recommendation as to method on an understanding of the nature of the mind is not to commit the error of psychologism, and such reliance does not confuse issues of logic with those of empirical science for the logic of discovery is not pure logic, but practical methodology.

A GAP IN UNDERSTANDING POPPER

Popper's personal decision to shift his efforts from the problems of the psychology of learning to the nature of scientific method has been justified by his masterful contributions to an understanding of scientific method. As we have seen, however, he went further than this, and minimized the role—and hence the importance—of his psychological theories.

Popper's attempt to segregate his logic of discovery from

---

7. Ibid., p. 52.

his psychology of discovery has had, we believe, a damaging effect on the understanding and appreciation of his work. First, because Popper played down his psychological theories and did not carry them further himself, the originality of his views—as explained in the previous chapter—has not been appreciated, nor has his psychological theory been further developed and tested. Secondly, the positive aspects of Popper's methodology, the principles which stimulate creative theorizing and testing, have been relatively neglected or not understood.

This latter point requires some explanation. Partly, no doubt, because *The Logic of Scientific Discovery* is organized around the demarcation principle of falsifiability, philosophers of science have tended to focus on such issues as how conclusive refutation can be, to what extent failed refutation is support of a theory, and whether there is some hidden inductive principle involved in falsifiability. For the most part they have rejected Popper's logical critique of induction, essentially, it seems, on the ground that since we think inductively there must be some viable logic of induction. Here, of course, they have not recognized that they are presuming a psychological theory (that of Locke and Hume) to which Popper has provided an alternative.

In contrast to this reception by philosophers of science (chiefly former members of the positivist Vienna Circle, and their students) Popper has generated great enthusiasm among many thinkers with whom he has had personal contact and among his own students. In fact, probably no other twentieth century philosopher (with the exception of Bertrand Russell) can boast so distinguished a list of admirers among scientists, including Nobel laureates such as Eccles and economist Friedrich von Hayek. But what excited these scientists and philosphers was not the technical detail—testability, 'corroboration' and the like—which Popper himself viewed as the least important aspect of his system of ideas. What they acquired, through reading or listening to him, were his non-inductive theory of learning and the positive spurs to research mentioned by Eccles: the importance of identifying and clarifying the problem, the value of bold conjecture and systematic testing and criticism, and the importance of making experimentation relevant to a problem and to theories.

These ideas are, of course, explicit in Popper's writing, but because he refused to connect them to his theory of the psychology of discovery—their actual source—and because of the space he devoted to technical issues, these central points of his methodology have not been appreciated by many readers. It is almost as if there were two traditions of understanding Popper: one an 'oral' tradition of a group—including some very distinguished thinkers—who have had contact with Popper, who take his learning theory as basic, and who are inspired in their own work by his principles of method; the other a 'written' tradition of readers from the positivist school, who are somewhat mystified as to what the fuss is all about. We hope that this book will help to close the gap in understanding.

SCIENTIFIC METHOD AND THE PSYCHOLOGY OF DISCOVERY

Popper's desire to segregate his theory of scientific method from psychological theory is by no means unique. Since the nineteenth century, many psychologists have wanted to separate psychology from philosophy and make psychology "scientific", and many philosophers in the twentieth century have been concerned to avoid psychologism. There has been an understandable motive on both sides: psychologists have wanted to stay clear of the vagaries, frustrations, and fashions that have characterized the history of philosophy; and many philosophers have been equally fearful of becoming mired in the elusive, difficult-to-characterize world of the subjective.

But however reasonable the motive, we think that the effort to segregate the fields of scientific method and of the psychology of learning—particularly the psychology of discovery—has been a regrettable error, with harmful consequences. Although the two fields are distinct, their problems are too intimately linked for one to ignore the other without detriment.

The methodology of science is essentially a practical subject concerned with the most productive methods of research and of the evaluation of theories and experiments. The psychology of learning and discovery, on the other hand, is concerned with understanding and describing the processes of learning and invention, and particularly with identifying the underlying laws and regularities that are involved in these processes. Because these subjects are prescriptive and descriptive sides of the same process, advances in one field will almost unavoidably have implications for the other. Science is one of the most outstanding examples of creative and innovative thinking, so that any full psychological theory of these processes must account for the methods of scientists, or at least be consistent with what has happened in the history of science. On the other hand, the best methods of research must be in harmony with the powers and limitations of the mind, and thus new discoveries about the psychology of innovation will raise new questions about the best methods of research.

This intimate relationship between the two fields means that some of the complications that psychologists and philosophers wanted to avoid do arise. For example, the question immediately arises: is Popper's psychology of discovery itself testable? If so, how does it compare with rival theories of learning and discovery? And what does the status of its tests say about the validity of the methods that Popper recommends? These questions and other difficulties raised by the closeness of the two fields are, in our view, much better faced than ignored. Artificially segregating issues of the psychology and logic of discovery has caused Popper's novel theory of trial and error to be neglected. And, indeed, the effort to segregate the two caused Popper to make some errors in his methodology, a subject we shall take up in Part II.

Within the main stream of psychology and philosophy, the damage has been greater. Psychologists, thinking they could steer clear of philosophy, have tended to assume an inductivist view of scientific method; this has led them to fix narrow, so-called 'behaviorist' limitations on their theorizing, limitations which have left open to many thinkers none but inductive psychological theories. Philosophers, particularly those of the positivist tradition, have on their part tended to presume the truth of the psychological theories of Lock and Hume, and this, in turn, has limited them to inductive methodologies.

We believe that in place of this destructive policy of segregation, each field should sustain a *critical awareness* of the other's work and of the mutual implications of it. In the remainder of this book we will attempt to foster such an awareness: first, by examining the implications of the novelty of Popper's psychology of discovery and of the close relationship of methodology and the psychology of learning; then by critically reviewing Popper's attempt to segregate the two fields and discussing the negative impact of this attempt on his standards for assessing scientific theories; and finally, after sketching a unified history of these closely related fields, we will reassess the current problem situation in the methodology of science and the psychology of learning.

PART II

CRITIQUE OF POPPER ON THE CONNECTION BETWEEN THE PSYCHOLOGY AND LOGIC OF DISCOVERY

3
POPPER'S STANDARDS
FOR SCIENCE

As we explained in the last chapter, Popper's submerging of his psychological theory has led to neglect of his ideas in psychology and to a misunderstanding of his methodology. But beyond this, his effort to keep his theory of scientific method independent of any theory of the nature of thinking led him to make what we feel are errors in constructing his methodology. These errors are not to be found in the positive guides to research that we have already mentioned, but rather in the *standards* Popper proposed as the means of indicating whether a theory can be considered acceptable to enter into scientific discourse and under what conditions a scientific theory should be rejected in the light of evidence. These standards constitute an important breakthrough in our understanding of the su-

41

periority of scientific methods, but they also contain unnecessary *rigidities* which are incompatible with Popper's insights in psychology and which should be rejected.

Popper's breakthrough was a theory explaining how empirical evidence and logic could guide the search for truth, even where all purported evidence and all theory is granted to be subject to error and open to fundamental revision. In this theory, Popper avoided both horns of a traditional dilemma, falling neither into a dogmatism—the belief that certainty is obtainable—nor into renouncing realism. Dogmatism was adopted, for example, by Edmund Husserl (1859–1938) and his followers in their attempt to find a secure basis for science. The positivists fell into a similar dogmatism in their belief in an incorrigible core of truth contained in observation, a core on which science could be securely based. And the traditional goal of describing reality was renounced by conventionalists and by many others who felt that there is a need for inductive verification or confirmation of scientific theories.

To appreciate the positive breakthrough made by Popper's standards for judging theories, let us briefly examine the alternative approaches—the horns of the dilemma—and then look at Popper's proposals. The two most important alternatives are what Popper has characterized as 'inductivism' and what Poincaré called 'conventionalism'.

INDUCTIVISM

The dominant British tradition in philosophy took as its point of departure the belief that Hume had solved the psychological problem of describing learning insofar as it need be done for purposes of understanding science. Therefore, the problem remaining for scientific method was to show that Hume's skeptical conclusions concerning the *validity* of induction were mistaken.

This switch to problems of validity had the immediate effect of divorcing British psychology from British philosophy. Such figures as David Hartley (1705–1757) continued to develop associationist psychology but they became far less important in British philosophy. Instead, the problems of scientific knowledge were thought to concern logic: it was not the psychology of induction which provided the key, but the logic of induction. Correctly spelled out, the logic of induction could show how we properly argue from observations to generalizations.

Acceptance of this view meant that philosophy became the study of methods of justification. For some philosophers, for example John Stuart Mill (1806–1873), the methods of justification were also the methods of discovery. Mill offered some now well-known methods of induction—the method of similarities and differences, for instance—which could at least provide the core of a solution to the problem of how induction itself, used as a method, could yield knowledge. It required some overriding faith in the uniformity of nature, but this faith could in turn be justified by induction. William Whewell (1794–1866), on the other hand, contended that true theories were identified by first forming a series of conjectures: when these conjectures were tested, the true ones would be confirmed and the false ones would eventually be refuted. The theories which survived testing could be presumed to be true.

By the twentieth century, however, these views of Mill and Whewell were recognized to be inadequate; it was perceived that the skeptical attacks on induction could still be mounted. So the problems remained open: philosophers still needed to justify induction and still had to find an inductive logic that was not so easily shown to be ineffective. The response to this problem was more Humean than ever: we would literally restrict ourselves to logic in debating theories, by discussing formal languages. Any statement which was not strictly about observations would be precluded from science. In a sense, the new program was psychology. It was a theory of meaning—that is, only verifiable statements were meaningful—but it called for a logic of inferences employing statements about sensation. It was a last ditch attempt to preserve Humean psychology *and* the belief that fully reliable knowledge could be obtained. The program gained considerable force because it was conservative, because logic was entering its heyday, and because an alternative to Hegelian idealism was being sought urgently by admirers of modern science.

Popper believed that the new approach toward a logic of induction had several serious flaws. He argued that the theory of meaning could not reasonably be upheld since, according to its own standard, it was meaningless; that the study of the logic of induction for formal languages could not yield a logic of induction for science; and that the logic of probability could not provide a theory of the probability of the truth of theories.

In attempting to provide an alternative to positivism, Popper at times fell into accepting positivist aims, such as minimizing the influence of metaphysics on scientific method. In developing his theories, he was guided by two sets of desiderata which were not always compatible. One set was that posed by his own psychology and his aim of explaining the growth of knowledge; the other, that imposed by the need to present arguments capable of convincing his chief opponents, the positivists. The second set had to contain desiderata that the positivists would accept as legitimate.

CONVENTIONALISM

At the same time as the evolution of logical positivism, there were developments in physics which threatened the whole project of describing the psychological processes which led to the learning of the certain truth. Newton's theories, which Kant had so confidently assumed to be certainly true, were being seriously challenged. Newton's particle theory of light had been overthrown in the early part of the nineteenth century, and developments in the theory of electricity and magnetism were threatening the Newtonian world view and even the specific claims of Newtonian mechanics and gravitational theory. These rejections of past scientific theories—which reached a climax with Einstein's theory of relativity—challenged thinkers to show how science could be considered superior to competitors such as superstition, magic, or pseudoscience.

One of the most impressive responses to this challenge came from Henri Poincaré (1854–1912), who argued that the change in theories in science does not signify the "bankruptcy of science"[1] because the most general theories are not to be taken as statements about reality which are simply true or false. Instead, they are a set of definitions convenient for classifying and describing observation. As new data appear, we may have to adjust our definitions, but there is no overthrow of theories; there is, rather, a continual adjustment and refinement of our scientific language so as to describe the results of experiment in a better way.

Poincaré's 'conventionalism' of course has its roots in an ancient attitude toward science. Those who for one reason or another were threatened by a literal interpretation of scientific theories—such as the Catholic church in the days of Galileo—have insisted that scientific theory should be considered as a mere convenience for classification, prediction, and so on. Others, such as Ernst Mach (1838–1916), have seen in conventionalism a way out of the dilemmas concerning induction: if general theories are

---

1. Henri Poincaré, *Science and Hypothesis*, p. 160.

just devices for 'mental economy', for conveniently sum-marizing data, then we need not question whether they can be relied on as true.

Though conventionalism was, and is, basically a defen-sive maneuver, Poincaré gave it a new life by inventing a conventionalist methodology. Freed to a degree from wor-ries about induction, he was able to explain the impor-tance of imagination in developing theories and of flexibil-ity in responding to new evidence. Unfortunately, the new methodology evolved by Poincaré had a restriction: the changes introduced in theory had to be gradual, step by step, in order to keep their roots in observation and exper-iment. This new conventionalist methodology of Poin-caré—and Pierre Duhem (1861–1916)—was to have a wide effect, particularly in the philosophy of physics; and his idea of the flexibility of mental frameworks was to influ-ence the psychology of Jean Piaget.

Though Poincaré revitalized conventionalism, it is still basically a failure as an attempt either to rescue the cer-tainty of science or to evade the problem of induction. Making scientific laws into definitions only rescues them as certain if they are, in principle, unresponsive to changes in data. If we acknowledge that new data may make an old definition with a given interpretation "inconvenient", as Poincaré would grant, then we may overthrow 'definitions' just as we did realistic theories. Similarly, the attempt to evade the problem of induction fails. All conventionalists grant that some kind of observation or observation state-ment has truth value, and the conveniences which are the-ories are used to *predict* certain results of observation and experiment. If we argue for the merits of one theory over another in its power to predict accurately, then we are making empirical claims, whether or not we acknowledge it. And these claims go beyond the existing data, just as do realistically interpreted theories. If we believe—as Poincaré does—that the theories somehow are justified by

experience, the problem again arises as to whether the justification is proper. Though we believe that conventionalism is a failure in its general aims, we should emphasize
that with Poincaré it broke new ground in both psychology and methodology by discussing the problem of how
theories and mental frameworks adjust and change under
the pressure of new information.

POPPER'S STANDARDS FOR ASSESSING
SCIENTIFIC THEORIES

To show that his view of scientific method was superior
to that of the inductivists and conventionalists, Popper
needed to supply a better solution to the problem that had
been of central concern to them: that of showing in what
better way current scientific theories stand up to the evidence of observation and experiment than do past theories
or theories outside science. For Popper, the better theory
would have to contain the lessons of his theory of learning: that induction does not take place, and that all observation is theory-impregnated and hence itself open to error.

The heart of Popper's answer, as we explained earlier, is
that the current scientific theories are falsifiable in principle and survive in the face of potentially falsifying observation and experiment, wheras the competing scientific
theories have been refuted by the evidence. Popper's standards for science, then, are that a theory may enter into
scientific discourse ("be seriously entertained"[2]) if it is
testable, that it be rejected if it has been refuted, and that
it be tentatively accepted if it has passed all tests. The lim-
iting factor is that, according to Popper's own view, the
potentially refuting evidence is corrigible: the apparent re-

2. Karl Popper, *The Logic of Scientific Discovery*, p. 31.

sult of an observation or experiment may be mistaken. Given the potential error in the observation report, when and why should we accept the observation report and reject the theory rather than the reverse?

In order to provide a better alternative to inductive and conventionalistic philosophies, Popper had to supply a theory of the acceptance of observation reports which would rely neither on induction nor dogmatism and which was not open to the skeptical charge of infinite regress. He did provide such a theory.

In Popper's view, the acceptance of basic statements is never forced, but rather is a free decision on the part of the community of scientific researchers. It is, however, a decision that is governed by rules. In particular, scientists try to discover results of observation and experiment that can be easily tested—for example, by repetition of an experiment—and they strive to come to agreement on the results of experiment. As Popper emphasizes, this effort to agree and to accept a particular result as (tentatively) correct is a *convention*, but it is a convention employed by scientists because it promotes discovery of the objective truth. Popper compares this decision to a jury's verdict: the agreement of the jury is not a proof of rightness, but it is governed by procedures designed to promote the discovery of the truth.

This concept of the acceptance of observation reports (or "basic statements", as Popper calls them) avoids any assumption that the scientists or "jurors" arrived at their decision by induction. And Popper, of course, with his view of the psychology of learning, would say that no such thing takes place, although he grants that scientists' subjective experience plays a motivating role in the initial stating and the eventual acceptance of a report. Popper's proposal also retains the realism of the scientific theory, which is not reduced to the level of a convenient 'convention'. He avoids as well, the skeptical charge of infinite regress; for even though the acceptance of a basic statement may be questioned *ad infinitum*, there is no claim that the acceptance constitutes final proof. Rather, the tentative inquiry serves a practical purpose: it helps us get closer to the truth. The stopping-point in the potential infinite regress therefore is not arbitrary.

Finally, the decision to accept basic statements is not dogmatic, in that it is tentative and open to revision in the light of further experiment, observation, and scientific theory. But Popper does emphasize that a kind of temporary dogmatism (our words) is desirable. It is here, in particular, that we believe that Popper goes too far. Let us therefore quote at some length what he has to say about the need to come to agreement on basic statements:

> Every test of a theory, whether resulting in its corroboration or falsification, must stop at some basic statement or other which we *decide to accept.* If we do not come to any decision, and do not accept some basic statement or other, then the test will have led nowhere. But considered from a logical point of view, the situation is never such that it compels us to stop at this particular basic statement rather than at that, or else give up the test altogether. For any basic statement can again in its turn be subjected to tests, using as a touchstone any of the basic statements which can be deduced from it with the help of some theory, either the one under test, or another. This procedure has no natural end. Thus if the test is to lead us anywhere, nothing remains but to stop at some point or other and say that we are satisfied, for the time being.
>
> It is fairly easy to see that we arrive in this way at a procedure according to which we stop only at a kind of statement that is especially easy to test. For it means that we are stopping at statements about whose acceptance or rejection the various investigators are likely to reach agreement. And if they do not agree, they will simply continue with the tests, or else

start them all over again. If this too leads to no result, then we might say that the statements in question were not inter-subjectively testable, or that we were not, after all, dealing with observable events. If some day it should no longer be possible for scientific observers to reach agreement about basic statements this would amount to a failure of language as a means of universal communication. It would amount to a new 'Babel of Tongues': scientific discovery would be reduced to absurdity. In this new Babel, the soaring edifice of science would soon lie in ruins.[3]

THE RIGIDITY OF POPPER'S THEORY OF STANDARDS

Though his theory of standards constituted a breakthrough, we believe that Popper made both his method of theory choice and his demarcation criterion too rigid. The key error in his method of theory choice is his apparent insistence on *consensus* on what basic statements are accepted as correct—that is, on the results of observation and experiment which are used to test theories. This demand for consensus also dictates agreement on what theories are to be rejected as refuted. Similarly, it induces a certain *unity of method* in scientific research because it does not allow disagreement (after initial agreement has been established) about whether a given bit of evidence refutes a theory. In the demarcation criterion, the rigidity lies in Popper's view that refutability is an *entrance requirement* for any theory to be considered for testing and development.

We believe that these rigidities are quite unnecessary and, in fact, will be harmful if they are adopted. To begin

3. Ibid., p. 104. Popper does not, of course, recommend consensus on theory or on programs for research, as Thomas Kuhn seems to do.

with, consensus on the results of experiment is not needed. Deductive logic, as Joseph Agassi has explained, may be used to evaluate the results of observation and experiment without any requirement of consensus.[4] He points out that we may designate an observation report either as true or as false. When we characterize the report as true, we attempt to deduce it from some theory and the conditions of the experiment; when we record it as false, we deduce the statement "such and such a (false) report was made," again from theory and the conditions we assume to have been the case. The key point made by Agassi is that explanations of false reports may be tested independently against alternative explanations, just as may alternative explanations of a report assumed by all to be true. For instance, our description of an erroneous report may include the assumption that the initial conditions of the experiment were misconstrued in a particular way. This assumption may be tested by reproducing the experiment, this time deliberately controlling the factor that was overlooked or misunderstood.

Given this possibility of the rational evaluation of evidence, diversity of opinion about the status of various experimental reports and theories is not so threatening. In reality, such discussion goes on frequently, and the diversity of opinion about theory and evidence has occurred historically and to the present day. Of course, if everybody had a totally different picture both of the evidence and of what theories are promising, cooperation in science would be nearly impossible. For this reason, search for persuasive evidence and persuasive interpretation of evidence is important. But Popper's insistence on agreement on basic statements is undesirable, for division of opinion on evidence can be fuel for fruitful critical evaluation of that evidence. In other words, the same rationale which Popper

4. Joseph Agassi, *Science in Flux*, pp. 110–115.

gives for bold speculation concerning theory—for the creation of fresh and various new ideas—applies equally to the effort to interpret correctly the results of experiment and observation.

Similarly, the degree of unity of method imposed by Popper is not desirable. Though we can present strong arguments for some methods being better than others, we cannot specify one rule overriding all others for the rejection of theories. Again, diversity may be more fruitful and, in any case, gives us the opportunity to evaluate methods themselves.

Generally speaking, we believe that any rule is misguided if it uniquely determines the choices of scientists.[5] Rules and techniques of research are invaluable, but they should be viewed as guides to choice rather than as full determinants of it. No single consideration should be paramount in guiding a task such as scientific research, where there are often great demands for imaginativeness and high risks of failure.

Popper's demarcation criterion errs, we believe, in making testability a prerequisite for any idea which is to be seriously entertained by science. There may be times when other considerations should override testability. For example, Agassi has pointed out that the fruitful strategy of taking a metaphysical, non-empirical idea and trying to make it testable is in conflict with Popper's recommendation.[6] Popper's requirement would bar a very productive method from discussion in science.

It must be admitted that Popper is aware that his methodological rules do not constitute a complete list[7]—that there are other rules which might be needed to prevent new conventionalist stratagems from undermining the demarcation criterion. He recognizes that the methodologi-

5. William Berkson, "Skeptical Rationalism", *Inquiry*, 22: pp. 281–320.
6. Agassi, *Science in Flux*, p. 219.
7. Karl Popper, *The Logic of Scientific Discovery*, p. 82.

cal (as opposed to the purely logical) side of the demarcation criterion "can hardly be made quite precise."[8] However, since he does not admit that there are any considerations which might legitimately overrule the aim of testability for a time, our point concerning excessive stringency holds. We contend that a consideration such as testability should be taken as only one of the goals of scientists (although an important one), rather than as a dictator of their choices.

POPPER ON THE RELIABILITY OF BELIEFS

One of the consequences of giving testability such an overwhelming importance in determining choices is Popper's tendency either to collapse all other considerations into testability or to regard them as peripheral. For example, in *The Logic of Scientific Discovery*, Popper argues that simplicity and testability are identical. And while admitting that metaphysics is sometimes an invaluable motivation for research, he makes it irrelevant to the actual methodology of research. The same tendency has operated on the issue of how we decide what to believe, and it is this issue which has been important to the reception of Popper's ideas among the positivists of the Vienna Circle and their followers, who in fact dominate the academic philosophy of science.

In the same book Popper carefully refuses to take a stand on the issue of reliability, on the grounds that subjective conviction is irrelevant to the logic of science.[9] However, in *Objective Knowledge* he reverses his stand, and claims that his theory of choice also applies to reliability. There are two main problems involved in the issue

8. Ibid., p. 88.
9. Ibid., pp. 44–47, 110.

of the reliability of belief: first, how do we arrive at our beliefs about what is reliable? and second, what beliefs is it proper (in some sense) to regard as reliable? Popper answers the first question as follows: "Are those 'strong pragmatic beliefs' which we all hold, such as the belief that there will be a tomorrow, the irrational results of repetition? My reply is: No. The repetition theory is untenable anyway. These beliefs are partly inborn, partly modifications of inborn beliefs resulting from the method of trial and error elimination."[10] Here Popper presents his theory fairly straightforwardly as psychological, especially as he calls the question in the quotation a "psychological problem of induction." However, again he protests that he is not really engaging in psychology: on the previous page he says," . . . I do not regard the psychological problem of induction as part of my own (objectivist) theory of knowledge."

Popper reformulates the question of what theory should be regarded properly as more reliable, as follows: "Which theory should we prefer for practical action, from a rational point of view?" His answer is that " . . . we should *prefer* as basis for action the best-tested theory . . . . The best-tested theory is the one which, in the light of our *critical discussion*, appears to be the best so far, and I do not know of anything more 'rational' than a well-conducted critical discussion."[11] And developing the same idea, Popper says: "More especially, a *pragmatic belief in the results of* science is not irrational, because there is nothing more 'rational' than the method of critical discussion, which is the method of science."[12]

Popper's stand on this issue is interesting in a historical perspective. He began with a psychological learning theory and altered it to a theory of the method of choice of sci-

10. Karl Popper, *Objective Knowledge*, p. 27.
11. Ibid., pp. 21–22.
12. Ibid., p. 27.

entific theories. This method of choice did not use notions of practical reliability at all. The positivists of the Vienna Circle, following Hume, saw the question of what theories can legitimately be regarded as reliable as the central problem of the theory of knowledge. They expected to see the problem addressed in *Logik der Forschung:* instead, they encountered claims of a solution to the problem of induction, but no discussion of reliability at all. Popper stated clearly that he didn't need a theory of subjective conviction for his method of theory choice, but the logical positivists do not seem to have understood the significance of this assertion.

One thing the positivists did not see was that Popper was addressing a problem different from theirs. His primary question was: how do we learn? His problem, therefore, was essentially one of discovery. The positivists' problem, on the contrary, was one of justification or choice of theories—not "How can I increase mankind's knowledge?" but rather, "In what theory should I put my trust?"

As we noted earlier, the positivists accepted Hume's psychological theory—that we learn by repetition of similar instances and with enough repetitions come to believe that a conjunction of events is a necessary connection or a universal law. The implication is that the learning of new ideas and coming to believe in them is one and the same process. The question that arises is: does this process lead us to believe in the right theories? The positivists could not accept Hume's answer that there is no sound reason to think that it does. Their need, then, was to find that sound reason.

Popper's approach to this problem was to reject Hume's psychology and replace it by conjectures and refutations. But once Hume's psychology is thrown out, the positivists' problem of what beliefs are reliable is no longer central to learning theory. In particular, Popper's belief that the heart of scientific method is the simultaneous use of bold imagination and severe criticism does not rest on any theory of reliability. This was another thing the positivists did not understand, and Popper could not point it out in a straightforward way because he could not describe his own theory of learning as a psychological one and discuss its consequences.

Popper's desire to show that we should believe in science had motivated him, we believe, to develop the criterion of demarcation. The same motivation lay behind the development of the theory of corroboration. Popper explains in *The Logic of Scientific Discovery* that such a theory is needed to distinguish the accepted scientific theories from the *"many theoretical systems* with a logical structure very similar to the one which at any particular time is the accepted system of empirical science."[13] These systems may be unrefuted and so would seem to be as good as existing accepted theory. Note that such theories pass both the demarcation criterion and (so far) all empirical tests.

Popper distinguishes scientific theories from the "very similar" ones by the (supposed) fact that they have a higher degree of corroboration. Theories are "corroborated" by verifying a basic statement which is a logical consequence of a theory. But those theories which are bold, which risk more, are assigned a higher degree of corroboration if they pass such tests. This turns out to be related to simplicity, so that many of the unrefuted theories similar to existing science are assigned lower degrees of corroboration. At any rate, this is Popper's intention.

Why is the more corroborated theory to be preferred over its equally scientific and surviving theory? The answer, it seems, is that we should believe in science—true

13. Popper, *Logic of Scientific Discovery*, p. 39.

science—and must be able to locate what to believe in. This, of course, is a conjecture about Popper's motive. It gains plausibility from the peculiar place 'degrees of corroboration' occupies in Popper's system. Agassi first noticed that it followed neither from the demarcation criterion nor from the underlying learning theory and proposed to throw it out. But Popper clung to it and for some time devoted his energies to developing it.[14] Despite development of the technical aspects of the theory, he did not really make clear what its purpose is. Our conjecture explains the anomaly: Popper wanted to develop the theory because it served his original aim of distinguishing the true and the false faiths of science. He could not say so because he saw that the 'belief' philosophies were misguided. Furthermore, it explains why positivists have settled on degrees of corroboration as a part of Popper's system that they can understand, and why they support Rudolf Carnap's contention that there really is little difference between Popper's position and his. They have correctly scented that, at bottom, corroboration concerns belief.

Popper was careful to avoid claiming that corroboration was intended as a measure of rational belief or of reliability. Still, he couldn't really reject his notion of corroboration completely and hold on to its original purpose. He shows a way out in his essay "Conjectural Knowledge": corroboration indicates rational preferability, a supposedly objective category, and not reliability or credibility.[15] However, it seems suspiciously like the measure of 'degree of belief based on evidence' which the inductivists were looking for.

Popper's claim that the best-tested scientific theory should be preferred as a basis for action is, we think, an

14. See the appendices to *The Logic of Scientific Discovery.*
15. Popper, *Objective Knowledge,* p. 13 ff.

unfortunate one. First, in effect it reunites the method of learning and the method of determining practical reliability which Popper has separated by his non-Humean psychology: if we learn by refutation, then increase of fully reliable belief and the increase of knowledge cannot be the same. Further, his claim implicitly requires that nonscientists believe in what scientists agree on. (Recall our discussion of the role of such agreement in the decision to regard a theory as refuted.) As well, it reinforces the erroneous idea that Popper did not take a direction fundamentally different from the ideas of the positivists. Finally, we believe it is wrong: reliability and scientific success are by no means in one to one correlation.

Let us examine this last point—that reliability and scientific success cannot be equated. Suppose we have two scientific theories, A and B, and that the new theory B reduces to a theory close to A under certain restricted conditions. Let us further suppose that this restricted area just happens to include all previous tests except a most recent one in which B clearly triumphed over A. According to Popper, theory B is clearly more successful as a scientific theory. Yet it would be a rash man who would say that we should immediately stop relying on A and start relying on B in all instances, even outside the restricted area. For example, dams may have been built using theory A, and these dams may have proved very reliable. But theory B says the dams will be much safer if they are built a different way. And the old theory predicts that the new-style dam will burst shortly after maximum water pressure is reached. Under the circumstances, to claim that future dams should be built to the specifications of theory B would be irresponsible. Popper's view ignores the ever-present gap between theory and practice.

To take a different type of case, suppose that a scientist from a prestigious university should tell me that he has scientifically refuted the theory that my neighbor of African ancestry should be treated as an equal, and that the vast majority of professors at other prestigious universities agree with his conclusion. I know, of course, that scientists have come to agreement on issues of race (for instance, in the German Nazi period) that were later discredited. But Popper's identification of reliability with scientific success tells me—quite contrary to his intention—that my most rational course is to believe what I am told.

A theory much more consistent with Popper's fallibilism would be something along the following lines: I, as an individual, try to sort out which ideas are true and which are false, so that I can act to best serve my aims. Similarly, the community of scientists tries to figure out which scientific theories are the better ones, to serve as a basis for improved technology (among other reasons). But among those ideas that I think are true, I regard some as more reliable than others. To gauge how reliable my own beliefs are, I have *standards to judge reliability:* for example, I think that my beliefs about the views of authors whose books I have read are more reliable than my beliefs about the views of authors whose books I have not read. In the same way, disciplines as diverse as the law and safety engineering develop opinions about which theories and which devices are more and less reliable.

These standards of reliability can be critically examined and, it is to be hoped, can be improved by trial and error, just as can scientific theories. Scientific success is, of course, one factor to be taken into account in judging reliability but, as our examples show, it is not the only one. We believe that Popper's error in identifying standards of reliability with scientific success is one he was forced into by his insistence that testability and testedness should override all other considerations.

THE CAUSES OF RIGIDITY AND THE CONFLICT WITH POPPER'S PSYCHOLOGY

The source of the undesirable rigidity of Popper's standards is probably threefold. First, Popper was (understandably) preoccupied with the problem of distinguishing and discrediting pseudoscience: in trying to ensure that it was excluded, he overlooked the fact that his standards had become too strict for much fruitful research. Second, he wanted to avoid relying on psychological theories, in particular his own, and probably believed that he could avoid such reliance if he could base methodology on a single rigid requirement. Finally, Popper did not have a theory—such as Agassi later supplied—explaining how to evaluate observation statements rationally. Here Popper was in the same boat as his mentor, Karl Bühler, and the other Würzburg thinkers: as we explain in Chapter Five, the policy of using introspection to test psychological theories foundered because the theories indicated that the reports of introspection would themselves be influenced by predisposing attitudes.

These three factors reinforce one another. Popper's desire for a sharp demarcation criterion made him reluctant to include psychological considerations. If psychology can influence methodology, we cannot require psychologists to stick rigidly to any methodology: the next psychological discovery may show the recommended methods to be inferior. In such a situation, a sharp distinction may not be possible. Popper was probably also reluctant to try to develop a theory of evaluating observation reports, since it would involve, for example, psychological theories of perception.

The influence operates in the other direction as well. If Popper wanted to avoid psychological considerations, he would have to produce some standard which, at least overtly, would override any such considerations. Similarly, lacking a solution to the problem of evaluating observation statements, he would be reluctant to include psychological considerations in evaluating his methodology.

We believe that these three concerns forced Popper to suppress his psychology (to resurrect it later as philosophy) and to put too tight a rein on the standards governing the acceptance or rejection of scientific theories. The same concerns prevented him from typifying his theory as clearly descriptive, prescriptive, or both. He usually defines his aim as that of characterizing the best methods of science. This keeps vague the issue of when he is to be counted as wrong in his descriptions, and it evades the question of whether he is trying to advocate what is best or if he has some independent standard of who practises good methods and is trying to describe those methods. In fact, Popper does put forward a standard of good scientific practice, he does think that many practitioners fall short of his recommendations, and he believes that most, if not all, of the greatest scientists have followed the methods he has articulated.

Again, these three factors prevented Popper from emerging more openly as a reformer, especially in *The Logic of Scientific Discovery*. Because he wanted to avoid appealing to psychological theory, he had to argue for his demarcation criterion, and for his methodology generally, on the vague grounds of "fruitfulness". Had he openly declared himself a reformer, he would have been called upon to explain more fully why the reforms are desirable. In order to avoid this explanation, he had to appeal to existing standards and to say, in effect, that he was simply making them clear.

Unfortunately, this appeal downplayed the innovative character of Popper's recommendation that boldness in speculation be combined with severity in criticism. Moreover, it encouraged Popper to compromise his own psychological theory, which in fact underlay his methodology, by regarding basic statements as 'atomic facts' for purposes of his methodology.

Though Popper emphasized strongly that basic statements were only basic in relation to a theory they were testing and that they were fallible and open to rejection, he used them in his method of theory choice in such a way that their tentative nature played no role. Except for his warning as to the relativity of basic statements, they retained the character of the discrete and unchanging elements which had been used by all associationists and even by the Würzburg school. The Würzburg theorists had a conflict within their psychological theory on this point because they, too, held that all observation was to be interpreted by thought and hence was fallible. Popper carried over this conflict without fully resolving it.

As we have explained, Popper has no positive theory of the rejection of observation reports. Moreover, as the following passage shows, he discounts the practical possibility of the rejection of basic statements:

> In general we regard an inter-subjectively testable falsification as final (provided it is well tested): this is the way in which the asymmetry between verification and falsification of theories makes itself felt. Each of these methodological points contributes in its own peculiar way to the historical development of science as a process of step by step approximations. A corroborative appraisal made at a later date—that is, an appraisal made after new basic statements have been added to those already accepted—can replace a positive degree of corroboration by a negative one, but not *vice versa*.[16]

The picture of the growth of science which Popper presents, then, is of a stable and increasing body of discrete

16. Popper, *Logic of Scientific Discovery*, p. 268.

facts against which successive theories are tested. Those theories which explain more facts and have no known counter-example supersede those with less scope or with some counter-examples. In order to supersede the old theory, they must contain some approximate version of it which will explain what the old theory was able to explain.

This picture of separate levels of singular facts and universal theories fits in with Hume's psychology but not with Popper's. For Popper emphasizes that psychologically there is no such thing as a "pure" fact, untainted by interpretation in the light of universal theory. He emphasizes, as well, that error and replacement can occur at any level. If we alter the picture to accord with his psychology, it is far less tidy. Since our view of what are the particular facts will change from time to time, the comparison of newer and older facts can be, as Paul Feyerabend has pointed out, a much more complex affair. As Agassi noted, we will have to use explanations of false reports as well as deductions of reports presumed true.

Aside from his simplistic account of the comparison of theories, Popper's view of basic statements as a stable background against which to test theories is in conflict with his important psychological theories and has served to bury them more deeply.

4
POPPER'S ATTEMPT TO FREE METHODOLOGY FROM PSYCHOLOGY

THE ATTEMPT
IN *THE LOGIC OF SCIENTIFIC DISCOVERY*

As we explained in Chapter 2, Popper argues early in *The Logic of Scientific Discovery* that the 'psychology of knowledge' is irrelevant to what he calls the 'logic of knowledge'—in other words, to methodology. Throughout the rest of the book Popper tries to argue for his principles of method without appeal to theories about the nature of thinking, including his own. His basic strategy is to derive the rules of method by means of the general principle that they are to be "constructed with the aim of ensuring the applicability of our criterion of demarcation." And though he admits that the connection of his methodological rules to the demarcation criterion "is not a strictly deductive or logical one,"[1] he still bases his arguments on it.

We believe that this attempt to base his methodology on the demarcation criterion fails. The importance of the criterion itself rests on Popper's view of the nature of learning, and without that basis the need to uphold it is no longer a compelling argument. Let us suppose, for instance, that the testability of theories was a distinguishing mark of science but only an incidental or even harmful feature. Even if it were a distinctive feature, it would be no basis for argument. One could equally well argue that since science has been historically more male-dominated than has literature, male predominance is a demarcation criterion. The importance of testability is not merely that it is distinctive but also that it is desirable as a feature of science.

Furthermore, testability would not be desirable if Popper were completely wrong about the nature of human thinking. If we contained an infallible light of reason or intuition, the truth would be obvious, and testability would be relatively unimportant. If, on the other hand, our minds were so weak as never to be able to originate a true theory, then testability would be only a depressing reminder of our limitations, not an engine of progress. It is only because of Popper's view of man as an active, imaginative, but very fallible solver of intellectual problems that testability is of central importance.

Even granting that testability is an important feature of science, the arguments Popper produces to support his rules of method do not hold up under scrutiny. That is because the rules go beyond minimally holding up testability and are aimed at taking *most* advantage of learning from error. This, again, is an aim that follows from Pop-

1. Karl Popper, *The Logic of Scientific Discovery*, p. 54.

66

per's view of the power and limitations of our thought processes.

In sum, when Popper's arguments are examined they turn out not to eliminate psychology at all, but rather to rest on Popper's own distinctive view of the nature of innovative thinking. Let us examine these arguments, case by case, beginning with those principles of method that seem most closely connected to the demarcation criterion.

The most closely related principle is the positive value that Popper places on refutation. He explains the practical force of this attitude by contrasting it with that of the conventionalists. When there is no crisis in an area of research, he explains, the conflict between his approach and theirs will not be apparent. However,

> it will be quite otherwise in a time of crisis. Whenever the 'classical' system of the day is threatened by the results of new experiments which might be interpreted as falsifications according to my point of view, the system will appear unshaken to the conventionalist. He will explain away the inconsistencies which may have arisen. . . . we [on the contrary] shall take the greatest interest in the falsifying experiment. We shall hail it as a success, for it has opened up new vistas into a world of new experiences. And we shall hail it even if these new experiences should furnish us with new arguments against our own most recent theories."[2]

This positive attitude toward refutations has two aspects. The first is the prohibition against evasion of refutation by *ad hoc* measures; the second is the recommendation to learn as much as possible from the refutation—to welcome it and explore the "new vistas" it opens up. The prohibition against *ad hoc* adjustments is the aspect

2. Ibid., p. 80.

most closely connected to the demarcation criterion, but even here the rule is not fully derivable. To ensure the applicability of the demarcation criterion, all that is required is that adjustments to existing theories be themselves *minimally* testable. A conventionalist could still fight a rear-guard action against the force of refutation without violating the requirement of testability. And though this kind of defence would, in Popper's view, be scientific, he would believe it not to be designed to best promote the growth of science.

When we turn to the recommendation to learn from error, the connection to the demarcation criterion becomes more tenuous. There is no reason, given the criterion of demarcation or even the method of theory selection by deductive testing, that we should expect a refutation to open up new vistas. It becomes clear only if we adopt Popper's view that important advances in knowledge involve the *correction* of old knowledge. Then we can see that the discovery of error may be a key stimulus to a new correction—which is a new advance—or that the particular correction may be a by-product of a new advance. In either case it is much to be welcomed. If, contrary to Popper's recommendation, we assume that correction of past errors is a negligible stimulus to research, we will not be so eager to seek refutations or so happy to find them. Thus we see it is Popper's theory of learning that underlies his positive attitude toward refutations.

Popper also tries to base his recommendations on the demarcation criterion in a second area of methodology, the theory of experiment. He proposes that instead of gathering observations and hoping a theory will emerge—as Bacon had recommended—we should first focus on a problem, evolve alternative theories to solve it, and *then* develop the experiment to test which solution is better. He explains this methodological priority of theory to experiment as follows:

. . . we should accept basic statements [only] in the course of testing *theories;* of raising searching questions about these theories, to be answered by the acceptance of basic statements. Thus the real situation is quite different from the one visualized by the naive empiricist, or the believer in inductive logic. He thinks that we begin by collecting and arranging our experiences, and so ascend the ladder of science. . . . But if I am ordered: 'Record what you are now experiencing' I shall hardly know how to obey this ambiguous order. . . . And even if the order could be obeyed . . . it could never add up to a *science.* A science needs points of view, and theoretical problems.[3]

Popper constructs an argument connecting his theory of experiment to the demarcation criterion. He begins by explaining that the acceptance of basic statements is done in accordance with rules, and then states that "of special importance among these is a rule which tells us that we should not accept *stray basic statements—i.e.* logically disconnected ones—but that we should accept basic statements in the course of testing *theories . . .*"[4] This rule, however, cannot be derived from the demarcation principle, though it is put forward as though it could. Popper seems rather to be repeating a rule mentioned earlier, also barring "stray" basic statements. This earlier rule *is* derived from the aim of preserving testability, but it has a different meaning; the basic statements are "stray" in a different sense.

He explains the earlier point thus: ". . . non-reproducible single occurrences are of no significance to science. Thus a few stray basic statements contradicting a theory will hardly induce us to reject it as falsified. We shall take it as falsified only if we discover a *reproducible* effect which refutes the theory. In other words, we only accept

3. Ibid., p. 106.
4. Ibid., p. 106.

the falsification if a low-level empirical hypothesis which describes such an effect is proposed and corroborated."[5]

But in the passage describing Popper's theory of experiment, what are called stray basic statements *do* have a logical connection to theory; namely, the contradiction of some theory. An example of the earlier stray basic statements is a report of sea serpents. This sense of "stray" is based on the demarcation criterion because what is in question is whether basic statements (as opposed to universal theories) are testable. Popper says basic statements are testable, and so part of science, only if we can specify conditions ("low-level" hypotheses) under which the effect can be observed by others.[6]

One might defend Popper's later usage of 'stray' merely as a strengthening of the earlier sense: if a basic statement has no logical connection to any theory, then there is no low-level falsifying hypothesis of which it is an instance, and it is unrepeatable. This is probably what Popper had in mind, and it does establish connection of the first part of his rule—not to accept logically disconnected basic statements—to the demarcation criterion. But it is not enough to support his main point; namely, the importance of first investigating alternative theories rather than first gathering facts. Thus the second part of his rule—that we should look for facts only as tests—does not follow; we can look for and record reproducible facts for the next century, blindly ignoring general theories or theoretical problems, without in the least violating the demarcation principle.

In reality, Popper's advocacy of experiment only as a means of testing and criticizing theories rests on his rejection of psychological learning theories which suppose that we learn by generalization from observation and upon his adoption of a learning theory which supposes that we

5. Ibid., p. 86.
6. Ibid., pp. 44–45.

learn by a series of conjectures and refutations. Because he believes that this is the fundamental method of creating new theories, he regards the collection of data unguided by theory as a waste of time. All of this concerns neither the demarcating of science nor particularly the method of choice of theory, but rather the methods of *invention* of theory and experiment. Again, because of his focus on the problems of demarcation and theory *choice*, his positive guides to research—in this case to fruitful experimentation—are not only given a faulty derivation but are also put into the shadow.

In the last pages of *The Logic of Scientific Discovery* Popper drops the attempt to derive his methodology from the demarcation criterion and instead eloquently describes his vision of the development of science. The emphasis is no longer on demarcation or on the decision to accept or reject a theory; rather it is on the quest for a better understanding of nature. Popper brings out here what is only briefly alluded to in the rest of the book—his belief that the heart of the scientific method is the combined search for bold theories and severe criticisms of those theories.

He describes theories as "marvellously imaginative and bold conjectures" which are "carefully and soberly controlled by systematic tests," and he goes on to say that

> our method of research is not to defend [these theories], in order to prove how right we are. On the contrary, we try to overthrow them. Using all the weapons of our logical, mathematical, and technical armoury, we try to prove that our [theories] were false—in order to put forward [others] in their stead. . . . The advance of science is not due to the fact that more and more perceptual experiences accumulate in the course of time. . . . Bold ideas, unjustified anticipations, and speculative thought, are our only means for interpreting nature: our only organon, our only instrument, for grasping her. And we must

71

hazard them to win our prize. . . . With the idol of certainty (including that of degrees of imperfect certainty or probability) there falls one of the defences of obscurantism which bar the way of scientific advance, checking the boldness of our questions, and endangering the rigour and the integrity of our tests. The wrong view of science betrays itself in the craving to be right; for it is not his *possession* of knowledge, of irrefutable truth, that makes the man of science, but his persistent and recklessly critical *quest* for truth.[7]

Popper's advocacy of boldness in conjecture and severity in testing is, as we explained in Chapter 2, a direct consequence of his theory of the psychology of learning. Could these cornerstones of Popper's methodology be derived from his logical analysis of testing? He makes no attempt to construct a derivation and, given the analysis of testing that he provides, it does not seem possible. At the beginning of *The Logic of Scientific Discovery*, Popper describes the problem of induction as the question "whether inductive inferences are justified, or under what conditions."[8] The problem he characterizes is one of *evaluation*, not creation, of theories or experiments. To argue for prescriptions about the search for new theories and experiments, we must take some stand on the processes by which innovation actually takes place: the psychology of discovery, the physical constraints on research, and the social structure of science. The logical analysis of testing and theory selection is not enough.

LATER DISCUSSION OF PSYCHOLOGICAL ISSUES

In the work he has published since *The Logic of Scientific Discovery*, Popper has explained his views on the psy-

7. Ibid., p. 279.
8. Ibid., p. 28.

chology of learning, and has developed them further. However, he has continued to insist on the complete independence of methodology from psychology. Furthermore, he has never put forward his psychological theories as such—that is, as scientific theories which can be developed and tested empirically. In fact, he has been persistently and even systematically inconsistent in this matter, sometimes denying that he is pursuing psychology and putting forward psychological theories in the same breath. Let us examine the nature of this inconsistency and then consider Popper's positive development of his psychological theories.

Popper's first published account of his psychology was the essay, "The Bucket and the Searchlight: Two Theories of Knowledge," from which we have already quoted. In it he puts forward his ideas as philosophy, and compares them to those of traditional philosophers such as Hume. He does not note that the theories he criticizes and to which he offers an alternative to would, in modern terms, be considered psychological. In the title essay of *Conjectures and Refutations*, he beautifully describes his psychological theories but goes on to say that aside from eliminating "certain psychological prejudices in favor of induction, my treatment of the *logical problem of induction* is completely independent of this criticism, and of all psychological considerations. . . . You may now forget my whole story [on psychology] with the exception of two logical points: my logical remarks on testability or falsifiability as the criterion of demarcation; and Hume's logical criticism of induction."[9]

This remarkable advice, probably directed as much to himself as to the reader, fortunately has been taken. But—as we have shown—it won't do. His method of critical testing, which he puts in place of induction, rests on

9. Karl Popper, *Conjectures and Refutations*, p. 52.

73

methodological rules; and these, as Popper acknowledges, are not purely logical. In fact, their rationale *is* the psychological theory at least as much as the principle of demarcation.

In his essay, "Two Faces of Common Sense," Popper says: ". . . I speak here of evolutionary epistemology, even though I contend that the leading ideas of epistemology are logical rather than factual [e.g., facts of psychology]; despite this, all of its examples, and many of its problems, may be suggested by studies of the genesis of knowledge."[10] And on the previous page he claims that ". . . logical investigation of questions of validity and approximation to truth . . . are in any case logically prior" to psychological questions. Thus Popper maintains his stance that the facts of human psychology will not be basic to the logic of scientific discovery.

That Popper has indeed put forward psychological theories, and in fact has felt them to be of fundamental importance, may be seen from his repeated return to questions of psychology and from his development of those questions.

One important elaboration of his psychology is the explicit introduction of *problems* into the theory. Popper had always felt that learning is problem-oriented, but it was only in 1966, in "Of Clouds and Clocks," that he made problems part of his *system*. In that essay Popper introduces the following characterization of the stages of inquiry: $P_1 \rightarrow TS \rightarrow EE \rightarrow P_2$.[11] Here P stands for problems, TS for tentative solution, and EE for error elimination. The changing subscript for P indicates that there has been progress from one problem to another new one. Popper of course realized that this was a departure and elsewhere[12] refers back to his paper, "What is Dialectic?" as an earlier

10. Karl Popper, *Objective Knowledge*, p. 68.
11. Ibid., p. 243.
12. Ibid., p. 164.

version of this schema. This claim is somewhat peculiar and shows, we believe, some confusion in Popper's mind about where problems fit into his system. The reference could equally appropriately (or inappropriately) have been made to *The Logic of Scientific Discovery:* equally appropriately because Popper refers there, as well as in the later essay, to problems as the *cause* of search for hypotheses; equally inappropriately because in that essay, as well as in other works, Popper does not take problems as an important component of the method of science—or, more generally, of the rational method. He characterizes his method as "conjectures and refutations", not as "problems, conjectures, and refutations".

The reason Popper shies away from the inclusion of problems as part of the method is fundamental: once problems are included, the method becomes a theory of the process of the *creation* of new ideas and not just (as Popper insisted in his first book) of their testing. Nevertheless, at crucial points Popper always refers to problems, because he actually *is* interested in the psychology of the invention of ideas, and because his theory was, in the first place, a psychological one.

How far Popper has retreated from the position he takes in *The Logic of Scientific Discovery* may be seen in his reply to Paul Bernays (1888–1977), who criticizes Popper's work for showing an "opposition of rationality and guess-work."[13] Popper admits that he has "perhaps gone too far" in saying earlier that "there is only one element of rationality in our attempts to know the world: it is the critical examination of our theories." But he quotes other passages in which he mentions problems, to show that the words "only one" were "not to be taken quite seriously."[14] This

---

13. Paul Bernays, "Concerning Rationality", *The Philosophy of Karl Popper*, ed. Paul Arthur Schilpp, p. 601.
14. Karl Popper, "Replies to my Critics", *The Philosophy of Karl Popper*, ed. Paul Arthur Schilpp, p. 1084.

defence is a little annoying: the statement is not the punch line of a joke; it is in as serious a tone as anything Popper has written. As we stated earlier, Popper is persistently inconsistent on this point, and there is no more reason for a reader to choose one inconsistency than to choose the other. Bernays's one consistent reading of Popper raised an issue which had in fact been Popper's central concern all along. Popper had already developed a most interesting theory of just what Bernays was asking for—a theory of the role of rationality in the creation of new ideas.

Popper openly replies, "I gladly admit that one should not overemphasize here the purely critical attitude, and that there can be such a thing as rational creativity or creative rationality."[15] This view is in sharp opposition to his statement in *The Logic of Scientific Discovery* that ". . . there is no such thing as a logical method of having new ideas, or a logical reconstruction of this process,"[16] and to his statement on the previous page (which we quoted earlier in this book) that "the question how it happens that a new idea occurs to a man . . . is irrelevant to the logical analysis of knowledge."

It is evident, then, that problems of psychology have been of primary importance to Popper, in spite of his repeated attempts to suppress them. In *Conjectures and Refutations* he presents his psychology as the "theory of knowledge", with reference to the classical views of Locke and Hume. In *Objective Knowledge* he continues to attack the problem of the psychology of learning but presents it under the guise of Darwinism.

By introducing problems as a component of the rational or scientific method, Popper has put the process of the invention of new ideas back into center stage. In *Objective*

---

15. Ibid., p. 1091.
16. Popper, *Logic of Scientific Discovery*, p. 32.

Knowledge he continues to develop a theory of how problems influence the thinking process. The theory involves two ideas which are worth examination: first, the objectivity of knowledge and logical relations; and second, the crucial importance of what Popper calls "Compton's Problem."

Problems and logical relations are 'objective', according to Popper, in that they can be regarded as independent of any particular thinker or any particular mental state. This independence is shown by the fact that we can speak of the logical consequences of a statement which no one has yet discovered. As we have seen in Chapter 2, Popper believes that the most important problems are contradictions between general theory and specific statements of observation. Since contradiction is a logical relation, this puts problems into the same objective category. Popper invents an ontological realm for these creatures, which he calls the realm of objective knowledge, or world 3 (world 1 is the physical and world 2 the mental world). Putting problems into world 3 frees Popper to discuss their role in the growth of science, for it permits him to skirt what we could call the question of interpretation—that is, of describing the mental correlate of problems and logical relations. Still, it is necessary to connect the relations in world 3 with thought processes in order to explain their impact on the growth of human knowledge. He has not proposed much in the way of a solution; rather, he has tried to formulate the problem in a way that will avoid the question of interpretation.

In his essay "Of Clouds and Clocks," Popper formulates two problems: he calls one "Compton's Problem," and the other "Descartes' Problem." Compton's Problem, which Popper says is "one of the most interesting problems of philosophy,"[17] considers how theories and plans can in-

17. Popper, *Objective Knowledge*, p. 231.

fluence our actions. In other words, it is the problem of how world 3, the world of objective knowledge, and world 1, the physical world, interact. Descartes' Problem deals with the interaction of the mental and physical worlds. Popper makes some interesting comments on a condition for solutions to either problem; he calls it "plastic control." He further tries to explain the utility, from the point of view of evolution, of the power of world 3 to influence world 1. His explanations, however, give neither the mechanism nor the laws of interaction of the two worlds.

The point we wish to note here, is that Popper avoids discussion of the interaction of worlds 2 and 3, the worlds of thought and objective knowledge. It is true that "Of Clouds and Clocks" was written before he had formulated the three worlds terminology; once this framework was in place, he did speak of the mental world of thinking as the intermediary between the physical world and the world of objective knowledge. However, he never develops a theory of interaction between the subjective and objective worlds, beyond saying that world 3 is a product of world 2, though independent after being produced. Instead he tries to minimize the role of the mental world as much as possible. For example, Popper's "main thesis" about world 3, in his "Two Faces of Common Sense," is that "almost all our subjective knowledge (world 2 knowledge) depends upon world 3, that is to say on (at least virtually) *linguistically formulated* theories."[18] However, it is clear that he feels that if he could develop a theory of the interaction between the two he would have something of great importance. He says, "I suggest one day we will have to revolutionize psychology by looking at the human mind as an organ for interacting with the objects of the third world; for understanding them, contributing to them, participat-

18. Ibid., p. 74.

ing in them; and for bringing them to bear on the first world."[19]

As we have seen, it was the absence of such a theory which turned him away from psychology and led him to formulate it as methodology. His realization that problems can be put into the objective category enables him to state his theory in a way which is closer to his original learning theory, but the difficulties he originally encountered continue to prevent him from putting it forward as psychology. He did, however, think of a way to use his methodology to make psychological claims. This is the idea of the 'principle of transference' from logic to psychology.

LOGIC AND PSYCHOLOGY

One difficulty Popper's psychological theory faced from the outset was the question of how his logical characterization of the learning process is related to the actual subjective process in the mind of the person thinking and learning. This relationship poses a particular problem for Popper because he has taken the 'formal' view of logic, a view most clearly expressed in the work of Alfred Tarski. According to this view, logic is a theory of the formal structure of sentences and inferences, and is independent of the particular content of the sentences. The study of formal structure has been carried out primarily for artificial languages, in which form and content are deliberately kept quite distinct. In these artificial languages the study of logic concerns the relation between form and *possible* content. For example, a valid argument is defined as one whose form necessitates a true conclusion when the meanings assigned to the terms make the premises true.

19. Ibid., p. 156.

Popper characterizes the upsetting of an expectation as a contradiction between a statement universal in form ("All swans are white.") and a statement singular in form ("There is now a non-white swan in the lake."). Since contradiction is, in the formal view of logic, a formal property of sentences, there is no such thing as a contradiction among ideas, expectations, or notions that have not been linguistically formulated. However, Popper believes that a child learns by conjectures and refutations before he learns language. And the experience of only being able to articulate a problem clearly after we have solved it is a common one. What, then, is the psychological correlate of the contradiction Popper describes? Under what circumstances do we feel the contradiction and when not?

Popper has indirectly addressed these questions by way of the three worlds metaphysics he has introduced into his writings since the mid-1960s. From one angle the metaphysics can be seen as a research program in psychology, where the analysis will be of the world 3 objects (including logical relations), and analysis of subjective consciousness can largely be avoided.

More specifically, Popper's essay "Conjectural Knowledge" introduces a new principle relating logic and psychology, the 'principle of transference.' He explains it as a kind of generalization of his earlier argument against Hume's theory of the psychology of induction:

> . . . I decided that Hume's inductive theory of the formation of beliefs could not possibly be true, *for logical reasons.* This led me to see that logical considerations may be transferred to psychological considerations; and it led me further to the heuristic conjecture that, quite generally, what holds in logic also holds—provided it is properly transferred—in psychology. (This heuristic principle is what I now call the 'principle of transference'.) I suppose it was this result

which made me give up psychology and turn to the logic of discovery.[20]

Earlier in the essay he characterizes the principle as stating that "what is true in logic is true in psychology" and says that "this is admittedly a somewhat daring conjecture in the psychology of cognition or thought processes."[21]

All this, unfortunately, does not resolve our earlier questions, but rather raises new ones. First, what is Popper talking about when he speaks of "what is true in logic"? The things that immediately come to mind are so-called 'logical truths' or 'tautologies'. These are statements whose logical form alone assures that they are true. For example, "All tables are tables" is a tautology. If this is what Popper is talking about, then the principle of transference is hardly a "daring conjecture," for logical truths, according to the formal view of logic, are true in all possible worlds. Furthermore, this view of logic is taken by Popper in his most careful consideration of the relations between logical and empirical statements, the essay "Why are the Calculi of Logic and Arithmetic Applicable to Reality?" There he says: "In so far as a [logical] calculus is applied to reality, it loses the character of a *logical* calculus and becomes a descriptive theory *which may be empirically refutable;* and in so far as it is treated as irrefutable, i.e. as a system of *logically true* formulae, rather than a descriptive scientific theory, it is not applied to reality."[22]

We might look to Popper's proviso "—provided it is properly transferred—" for help, but it is of no use: Popper does not say what "proper" transference is. In a wide sense it would mean only that those formulas of mathematics and logic which are changed into empirical conjectures are

20. Ibid., p. 26.
21. Ibid., p. 6.
22. Popper, *Conjectures and Refutations*, p. 210.

81

"correctly" changed whenever they are true—and this is not very enlightening.

A set of examples would also be helpful in understanding the principle of transference, but we have little to go on. The only example given is the critique of Hume, and here the role played by principles of logic is problematic. As we explained in Chapter 1, Popper's critique rests on two premises: the empirical fact that repetition is not exact, and the logical point that anything can—with a suitably defined predicate—be considered a repetition of anything else. But here the argument is, first of all, based not only on a point of logic, but also on a feature of our world. Furthermore, the force of the argument seems to come mainly from observation about the world: if repetition is not exact, then we must have a point of view or a theory to select what is a repetition. The inexactitude of repetition seems enough to make Popper's point.

Popper, however, claims that the argument shows that the points of view are "logically prior . . . to repetition."[23] It is not clear what he means by "logically prior." Is he claiming that in setting up a formal language we cannot take the term "repetition" as a primitive one but must define it in terms of some universal statements? This claim would be questionable in any case, but Popper does not defend it or further explain the meaning of "logically prior."

An effort to understand the principle of transference is further complicated by Popper's apparently contradictory accounts of the reason he switched from psychology to the 'logic of discovery'. We have recently quoted him as attributing it to a realization of the value of the principle of transference, but in his autobiography he seems to attribute it to a recognition of the *misguided* character of attempts to apply transfer logic to psychology:

23. Popper, *Logic of Scientific Discovery*, p. 422.

Giving up the psychology of discovery and of thinking, to which I had devoted years, was a lengthy process which culminated in the following insight. I found that association psychology—the psychology of Locke, Berkeley, and Hume—was merely a translation of Aristotelian subject-predicate logic into psychological terms. . . . A further step showed me that the mechanism of translating a dubious logical doctrine into one of an allegedly empirical psychology was still at work, and had its dangers, even for such an outstanding thinker as Bühler.

Admittedly Popper says that his conclusion from all this was a belief in the *"priority of the study of logic over the study of subjective thought processes."*[24] However, the hostility indicated in this quotation seems directed toward the process of transference itself. Of course, we have the qualifications of "dubious" logical doctrine and "allegedly" empirical psychology, but this doesn't help us: Popper never tells us what logic *he* is using, much less how dubious it is.

In sum, Popper has not provided a theory of the psychological correlate of a contradiction between a universal and a singular statement; and the principle of transference, in so far as we can understand it, seems not to be a clear principle at all, but rather a name for an absent theory.

24. Karl Popper, "Autobiography of Karl Popper", *The Philosophy of Karl Popper*, ed. Paul Arthur Schilpp, pp. 60–61.

PART III

REASSESSING THE PROBLEM SITUATION

5
THE HISTORY OF THE INTERACTION BETWEEN THE PSYCHOLOGY OF LEARNING AND THE PHILOSOPHY OF SCIENCE

Our perception of present-day problems is largely conditioned by our perceptions of the strengths and weaknesses of past intellectual efforts. In this chapter and the next we will recast the modern history of the philosophy of science and the psychology of learning into a single account: the story of the attempt to understand how innate factors and experiences interact in the learning process.

We will trace the development of methodological and psychological theories from Bacon to Hume and then to two traditions which sprang from Hume's research: the British tradition of attempts to solve the problem of induction, and the German tradition of attempting a psychological explanation of how knowledge is attained. This latter tradition was begun by Kant, and we will follow it from

Kant to Helmholtz, to Wundt, to Külpe, and finally to Karl
Bühler, who was Popper's teacher.

BACON AND THE METHOD OF INDUCTION

In his *Novum Organum* Francis Bacon (1561–1626) pro-
claimed that there was a method of induction which could
produce a new science. Bacon assumed that we have both
the innate ability to make inductions from the facts and
the inborn ability to recognize facts and true generalizations when we see them. His central concerns were to explain why, in spite of these powers of the mind, erroneous
beliefs were widespread and persistent; and to provide a
theory to assure that only *certain* truths would be adopted.
His solution to the first concern was his famous doctrine
of prejudice or of 'idols of the mind', his psychological
theory of error.

According to Bacon, the source of error is hasty generalization followed by vain attachment to the theory we
have created. The cure for this tendency is threefold: first,
to purge the mind of all preconceived theories; second, to
collect facts observed with the mind still free of preconceived theories; and finally, to make inductions from the
facts, taking care not to go too far beyond them. In the
second book of *Novum Organum,* Bacon added to these
basic steps a method of induction by elimination: once the
mind had been purified, many hypotheses could be in-
vented, and those incompatible with the facts could be rejected, with the true theory remaining.

Bacon's doctrine of prejudice and his theory of induction
by elimination do not sit well together because one proposal views conjectures (hasty generalizations) as a mal-
function of the mind, while the other views them as natural, even universal, occurrences. Nevertheless, both the

doctrine of prejudice and idea of induction as the basis of science became generally accepted. Bacon's writings themselves did not provide a coherent or convincing account of either scientific discovery or of proof. In particular, the psychology did not describe the operations of the mind, and the methodology failed to notice the problems of induction: Bacon presumed that the innate ability to "see" the truth assured the validity of induction. Because of these weaknesses, those who accepted Bacon's basic emphasis on proof by observation attempted to improve upon his ideas. His most important immediate follower was John Locke.

LOCKE AND THE PSYCHOLOGY OF INDUCTION

John Locke had the idea that we could separate certain knowledge from mere opinion if we knew the process of origin and genesis of our ideas. Concerning this origin, Locke agreed with Bacon on two crucial points: first, that we have the capacity to make inductions from pure observation; secondly, that error is the result of using ideas insufficiently proved by observation. Locke's problem was, in effect, to provide a psychological hypothesis adequate to describe the Baconian process of the creation of scientific theories. He developed a psychological theory which was distinguished by its insistence that all knowledge was derived, directly or indirectly, from sensation. Our ideas are not all directly derived from sensation, according to Locke: some are the product of reflection. Reflection is the perception of disagreement or agreement with the ideas we receive from direct observation of the outside world. Beginning from this basic position, Locke tried to account for the development of our knowledge in almost every area of thought.

89

In developing his psychology Locke did not adhere consistently to his commitment to sensationalism. He was first attacked for this inconsistency by Bishop George Berkeley (1685–1753), who argued that the notion of material substance (accepted by Locke) was really a meaningless concept because it was not derivable from sensation. However, it was David Hume who tried to work out a new psychology resting on a purely sensationalist basis.

HUME AND THE BREAKDOWN OF THE LOGIC OF INDUCTION

Hume shared Locke's aim of developing an associationist psychology that can explain how we have knowledge by induction, but he did not want to incorporate the non-sensationalist assumptions made be Locke. Not only was his problem the same, he followed the same procedure: he attempted to develop a psychology which shows how we obtain knowledge. At some point, however, Hume's aim differed. He wanted to show that if the now well-accepted associationist psychology were rigorously developed, knowledge (i.e. justification) could not be obtained. In one respect Hume is the most successful philosopher in our story, in that both the British and the German tradition arose from an effort to show that he was wrong.

Hume developed his psychology from two basic distinctions. The first is the distinction between immediate sense impressions and what are supposed to be their copies, namely, ideas. Everything we are conscious of is either an impression or an idea, and it obviously follows that all knowledge is derived from sense experience. The second distinction is that between the simple and the complex. Simple impressions or ideas are atomic, i.e. indivisible. Complex impressions or ideas are *associations* of the simple ones; moreover, we can have associations of complexes into larger ones. The main problem of psychology for Hume, then, was by what rules association takes place.

He solved the problem with a simple and brilliant theory. All association is due to one of three reasons: resemblance, contiguity in time or space, or cause and effect. Hume assumed that the perception of resemblance and contiguity posed no problem. He attempted to explain cause and effect in terms of contiguity. His theory, as we have discussed in an earlier context, is that the effect of one event repeatedly following another in time and place induces in us a belief that there is a necessary connection between the two. However, he had to conclude that the belief could not be justified—that is, proved by experience. Any belief in necessary connection goes beyond experience we have had, for it makes assumptions about the future. Because past experience cannot verify these beliefs, the assumption of necessary connections must remain unjustified.

The story has come full circle. Bacon had proposed a theory of scientific method in which the method of discovery, being based on observation, ensures the correctness of the theory. Locke attempted to explain the psychology of the Baconian method in order to clarify what knowledge could be regarded as certain, scientific. In making Locke's psychology consistently sensationalist, Hume came to the conclusion that the belief in scientific laws of nature is quite irrational (though, he thought, inevitable).

Thinkers interested in the problem of how we learn the truth reacted in different ways to Hume's work. Some, such as John Stuart Mill and the modern logical positivists, assumed that Hume's psychology is correct and attempted to show that his conclusion is wrong. They tried to provide a positive theory of how such belief is justified. Others, beginning with Kant, rejected Hume's psychology. They tried to produce an alternative account of the psychology of learning and to solve the problem of how we learn the truth by using that alternative account.

KANT: AN ALTERNATIVE TO ASSOCIATIONISM

One of the crucial questions for nineteenth century German philosophy and psychology was: how can scientific psychology be carried out? Kant's work introduced considerable complexity to the issue, for his solution to the problem of epistemology made the whole field of psychology problematical. Let us examine his views.

Kant saw clearly that universal laws could never be proved if the only source of knowledge is sense experience. Since he also assumed that learning in science meant learning the certain truth—and he believed in the certainty of Newtonian science—he concluded that there must be sources of knowledge (which he terms *"a priori"* sources) which are valid independent of experience. Kant puts the problem and his solution thus: ". . . Experience never confers on its judgments true or strict, but only assumed and comparative *universality*, through induction. . . . If, then, a judgment is thought with strict universality . . . it is not derived from experience, but is valid absolutely *a priori.*" For example, our ideas of cause and effect contain the concept of "the strict universality of the [causal] rule," and so the notion of cause "would be altogether lost if we attempted to derive it, as Hume has done, from a repeated association of that which happens with that which precedes. . . .": such a derivation would give to the rule only a "subjective necessity."[1]

All valid universal judgments, then, derive from a source of knowledge outside experience. This source is our inborn mental framework, which according to Kant con-

1. Immanuel Kant, *Critique of Pure Reason*, p. 44.

tains such concepts as causality. We use it in actively interpreting our sensations; in fact, all experience is the result of marrying sensation with the internal framework. For example, Kant claims that we do come to believe in particular causal laws as a result of seeing the repeated association of certain observations. However, that belief is not derived from sensation alone, but also from the category of causality, which we use to interpret sensation.

Basically, then, Kant says that the only certain universal laws are those inherent in our mental framework, and that they are the principles by which we organize experience. They do not provide any knowledge of the thing-in-itself. These views had implications for the possibility of a scientific psychology. First, any theory of the thing-in-itself cannot be certain, i.e. scientific, yet Kant's approach forced him to presume such knowledge as a presupposition of the knowledge that we actually have. The question then is: are such presuppositions knowledge—even though not part of our innate framework for experiencing the world—or are they simply subjective? Such Kantian 'ideals' as God and beauty are threatened by this problem, and so psychology as a study of the ego must be ruled out.

The second possible way of carrying out scientific psychology is to identify the innate framework we use to order our perceptions as humans. This, also, was impossible for Kant. Though there are elements of interpreted sensations which are ordered by frameworks, the principles organizing them already are identified as laws ordering things in space and time, i.e. the laws of physics. This leaves to psychology only the province of sensation either *not ordered* or *not yet ordered*, which is subjective and cannot be studied scientifically.

Such considerations led Kant to deny the possibility of any mathematical laws of our actual experience. This rejection of scientific psychology was the result of Kant's presuppositions about knowledge. His presumption that knowledge must be certain forced him to make all knowledge *a priori*, and thus to make the study of knowledge the study of our mental frameworks. This, in turn, became the only possible psychology. Yet his theory did not provide the scientific empirical psychology which by traditional standards and common tradition was thought to be needed. He left no scientific account of human purpose, could not distinguish scientific from transcendental psychology, could not distinguish physics from psychology. He made all mistakes private, since anything public would be scientific, i.e. certain.

These deep and far-reaching problems in Kant's philosophy were important for nineteenth century philosophy and psychology. Theorists in the German-speaking world accepted the need for an explanation of how knowledge grows through the partial use of frameworks and a psychological theory of how these frameworks are originated and grow or change. This, indeed, was the task of the line of philosopher-psychologists we will now discuss.

MÜLLER

The influence of Kant, of course, was very great on both those who attempted to confirm his ideas and those who tried to refute them. One reaction was the effort made by the idealist philosophers Johann Fichte (1762–1814), Friedrich von Schelling (1775–1854), and G.W.F. Hegel (1770–1831) to derive almost all basic theories of the world by *a priori* analysis. Most thinkers sympathetic to Newtonian science felt these men were setting up a sterile and pernicious rival to science. Their influence was mainly negative: philosophers of science felt called upon to answer the idealist challenge by showing what the distinctive and superior methods of science were. This concern became a dominant one in the twentieth century, both for the logical positivists and for Popper.

Johannes Müller, a follower of Kant, made the first significant attempt to show (in reaction to Kant) how an empirical and scientific psychology could be possible. He made the study of psychology the study of the physiology of the nervous system. This opened the way for the study of psychology, because physiology was believed a subdiscipline of physics, and hence scientific.

His problem was to show that physiology can provide interesting (psychological) theories, and initially he was very successful. For instance, he discovered that each nerve has a specific function; that is, that one nerve can conduct only one kind of sensation. Such physiological discoveries were of considerable importance. He combined them with the serious psychological hypothesis that mental frameworks, precepts, and so on, are innate, and that the physiology of these innate activities can be used to explain them. The hypothesis turned out to be false, and Müller's Kantian innatism was rejected (for other reasons as well) as being too strong.

Müller's research encouraged a great increase and development of physiological psychology. It was to be continued in the work of his student Helmholtz, but his view of the task of physiological psychology was rejected. Nevertheless, the hypothesis did not die: Wilhelm Max Wundt (1832–1920), Helmholtz's assistant, resurrected it as a basis for his 'physiological psychology'.

HELMHOLTZ

Helmholtz had the highest praise for Müller's work, and he was no doubt indebted to Müller for showing the way toward the valuable work in physiology that Helmholtz was to conduct. Helmholtz broke away, however, from

Müller's hypothesis of the innateness of conceptions of objects.

In doing so, he was simultaneously breaking away from Kant and developing an impressive theory of perception—a theory that perception is learned. This new concept left the door open for continued studies in physiology and, for a scientific psychology as well; that is, for a law of the formation of our conceptions. Helmholtz was aware that such laws were not then available, and he knew they would not be easy to form.

Let us first discuss Helmholtz's break with Kant and Müller. He accepted Kant's answer to Hume on causality—that is, he believed that we have an innate concept of cause which we use in interpreting observation. But the other concepts which Kant had claimed are innate are, according to Helmholtz, learned. The concepts of geometry, for instance, are learned, although this learning is supposed to be in some ways different from that proposed by Hume. Because Müller had adopted Kant's theory of innate concepts, Helmholtz's rejection of the theory is also an attack on Müller's psychology of perception. Helmholtz wanted to show that our immediate perceptions of objects are learned, and he held that experiments in the perception of objects do not yield—as the innatist theory would predict—constant perceptions in the same circumstances.

Helmholtz's criticism of Müller is also a criticism of the sensationalist-associationist view (which he refers to as 'Lockean'), according to which there are given signs which we learn to interpret via associations. In Helmholtz's view, even though perception is of objects, it is learned. We learn by rapid inductions from sensations which cannot be described. We use such conceptions in perception and improve them through a process of verification, in much the same way that scientific theories are verified. The access to the rules of this process appears doubtful, however, since we cannot even describe the elements; all perception involves memory.

The key to the difference in Helmholtz's view lay in the great role that 'unconscious inference' was supposed to play in perception. One example Helmholtz gives is of the sensation of a grain of sand between two fingers. If the two fingers are pressed together, we sense one grain of sand between them; but if the fingers are apart, we will interpret the one grain of sand as two. The example illustrates two points: first, that the perception of a grain of sand must be *learned*, just as one must learn a language; second, that the memory of what we have learned acts rapidly in an unconscious inference from the sensory inputs to what we consciously experience.

Helmholtz argues the same points from the existence of the limitations in our sensory apparatus. The eye, for example, displays a blind spot and certain kinds of color distortion, but we learn how to adjust to these limitations and to interpret more accurately what we see. We do this instantaneously, without having to think about it; we simply learn to sense things differently.

Helmholtz's demonstration that we *learn* to perceive, and that memory strongly conditions our perception, shattered both Kantian and Humean psychology. On the one hand, it showed that perception could not merely be the marrying of an inborn framework with external stimulus. The framework which conditions perception is a growing and changing thing, and its growth is influenced by earlier perceptions. On the other hand, neither could Hume's psychology be correct. It is true that Helmholtz viewed the unconscious inference and the learning involved in perception as *induction* from particular inputs to the actual perception, but this induction could no longer meet the requirements of Locke or Hume. Helmholtz's work contradicts Hume's idea of a mere association of simple elements. Our immediate impression of an object, for example, is not merely a sum of the particular qualities which we see: memory of what we have learned intervenes, so that there is no simple correspondence between the particular aspects of our sensory input and what we actually see. For example, we are not ordinarily aware of the blind spot: when we move our eyes, we see a continuous picture with no missing parts.

Helmholtz's work also attacks Locke's system for discovering which ideas are correctly or incorrectly derived from experience. For Helmholtz, there is no simple correspondence between our perception of an object and the qualities of the object itself. What we see is caused by a real object, but the exact similarities and dissimilarities must be a matter for empirical research, and there is no simple solution such as Locke wanted. In other words, a particular relation between our perceptions and external objects cannot be presupposed as a basis for inductions in science: it must be a subject for scientific investigation. But this throws into doubt the whole project of showing that we learn the truth by proper inductions from reliable observation, for if so much interpretation goes on, the observations may be unreliable.

Initially, however, philosophers and psychologists were unwilling—as was Helmholtz himself—to draw such radical conclusions from his work. We suspect that they were unwilling to consider that science might be less than fully reliable knowledge. The theory of the inductive verification of scientific theories seemed to Helmholtz to be straightforwardly applicable to the verification of our conceptions of objects. However, its effect on most of those who assumed that fully reliable knowledge must exist was to drive them back to Kant or Hume. Ernst Mach, for example, wanted to provide a firm basis for physics by analyzing sensations into their constituent atoms or 'elements'. He was followed in this effort by Bertrand Russell and then by the logical positivists. In another direction,

Edmund Husserl tried to develop a kind of certainly true transcendental psychology—as Kant had—again to provide a firm basis for all science.

Helmholtz realized that his researchers were of considerable importance for the philosophy of science, but his philosophical response was inadequate: he maintained the major tenets of the inductivist philosophy of science. In order to uphold the old views, he distinguished two kinds of learning. The first kind is scientific: it is obtained by expressing theories in a clear fashion and by testing and confirming them by means of deductions. In theoretical science we can understand why we came to particular conclusions, and we can lay out our arguments and go over them to assess their accuracy. The second kind of learning is the learning of sensations. We learn correct sensation by the use of our memory and by rapid changes of thought and patterns of recognition—changes too complex and rapid to be put in the definite form of scientific theories, and which cannot, therefore, be evaluated in the same way. Nevertheless, memory and learning serve to provide us with increased accuracy of sensation.

Helmholtz's response was inadequate because it employs a Humean theory of perception, according to which we learn to correct perception simply by memory and some unexplained process. Helmholtz acknowledged that he does not explain very fully how this process comes about: nevertheless, to the extent that he does explain it, he is Humean. Moreover, his response is deficient because it distinguishes sharply between our theoretical knowledge and our perceptions. In doing so, it saves both the independence and the reliability of observation, but if our theories shape the way we perceive the world, so sharp a division seems implausible.

So Helmholtz's theory leaves us with some serious problems. First, there seems to be a psychological process of learning which is not yet described, but which needs to be.

Like Kant, Helmholtz believes that science is incapable of describing the mental process or associating sensations. Secondly, there is a question that Helmholtz ignores: Is a theory about perception psychological only, or is it also methodological? Further, the process of perception is no longer connected to our learning of theories or to our learning of science in any clear-cut way; although since observation depends on theory, such a connection needs to be made. And finally, these problems raise doubts as to how we can understand the world at all—why these processes enable us to achieve any correspondence between an objective world and our theories, which no longer have any reliable touchstone.

The problems raised by Helmholtz's work led directly to the concerns of many theorists, including Wundt, Gustav Fechner (1801–1887), Külpe, Bühler, the Gestalt psychologists, and Selz. One approach to dealing with these problems attributed increase in learning to the incorporation of the theories of learning (associationist) and perception (non-associationist) into one unified theory. As we will explain, the program did not work. (Indeed, we believe that all the attempts to combine associationism—the most prominent learning theory—and Gestalt—the most prominent perception theory—have failed.)

A second group of theorists, following the line Helmholtz had taken, attempted to separate perception theory from learning theory while still maintaining the non-associationist learning theory. They supported the view that learning requires the attainment of true theories; thus these learning theories were capable of explaining very little. This approach allowed one to limit the impact of the non-associationist discoveries in the theory of perception.

A final proposal attempted to develop the perception theory in an associationist fashion. This was the major thrust of the program of scientific psychology led by Fechner and Wundt in response to the contention of Kant (and

100

then Helmholtz) that the association of sensations could not be scientifically described. It was Külpe's early participation in this effort, and his subsequent conclusion that Kant and Helmholtz were right in their critique, that led to the quest for a new, non-associationist psychological theory.

WUNDT

Wundt was in various respects a follower of both Kant and Helmholtz. However, he advocated the study of psychology as a science, a proposal that both men would have repudiated. The principal significance of his thought for our story is his theory explaining how psychological research can be made properly scientific. Neither the actual "scientific" results nor his other philosophical work need examination here, so let us begin with the core of his theory.

Wundt agreed with Kant and Helmholtz in viewing the mind as active. He held that there is an act of apperception which unites various elements of perception in a single, unitary, non-divisible perception. This perception is not, however, a function of *a priori* concepts; rather—coming closer to Müller's view—it is a product of a *physiological* process which results in apperception.

Helmholtz also believed that such units of apperception exist, but he claimed they were learned, a product of memory and rapid association which could not be analyzed. He thought that they could not (yet) be studied empirically because the processes could not (yet) be studied. Wundt solved this problem by theorizing that the process of combination is not the result of learning and judgment, but is physiological. For example, even though a color may be analyzable into more fundamental colors, the physiological mechanism of perception can analyze only the combined effect. He contended that the proper study of psy-

101

chology is this physiological mechanism. (The impossibility of analyzing perceptions into component stimuli was the basis of his criticism of Fechner's psycho-physical parallelism; the analysis of physical entities does not correspond to analysis of psychological ones.)

Wundt's physiological hypothesis allowed for scientific psychology. The study of physiology obviously is scientific. Wundt proposed simply to study how this physiological process produces psychological processes which can be studied as correlates of the physiological ones. Such a study also could lend itself to mathematical treatment, because the physiological processes could be measured quantitatively. Helmholtz and Müller already had led the way in the endeavor to study the physiology of the nervous system: Wundt simply wanted to extend this study.

The method that he proposed was introspection. We can observe our thought, feelings, and perceptions under circumstances described physiologically, study the psychological correlates of the physiological processes, and describe them with psychological laws. The Fechner-Weber law was the most significant product of this method: it states that the strength of the perception increases as the logarithm of the stimulus. Wundt endorsed the law, but disagreed with Fechner on the interpretation.

Fechner believed that the law shows a correlation between physical events—the stimuli—and mental events: that it demonstrates the nature of psycho-physical parallelism. Wundt, on the other hand, gave it a psychological-physiological interpretation: that it shows how the physiology of the nervous system responds when it is called upon to compare stimuli. Wundt contended that when there is an absolute measure on both sides, rather than on the physical side alone the increase will be not logarithmic, but linear.

Another way of stating this disagreement is that Fechner thought that 'just noticeable differences'—j.n.d.'s—

were an absolute measurement which could be correlated with external stimuli. Wundt thought that j.n.d.'s would depend on the complex stimuli, including such factors as comparison united in apperception as a result of the physiological mechanism. The law nevertheless had wide application, because most perceptions were comparative; that is, complex apperceptions.

Wundt and Fechner both believed that the future of scientific psychology lay in the inductive discovery of laws such as Fechner's. The greatest challenge was to extend the study of rudimentary or sensitive apperception to the higher thought process. Regardless of how one views Fechner's law (and today it is not highly regarded because the unit of measurement—the j.n.d.—is vague), Wundt's program was not successful. The researchers failed to discover the laws of the association of elements of apperception that they sought.

There were at least two significant reactions to this failure. Many of Wundt's students were Americans, and they changed the program from the quest for laws to the description of individual differences. They kept Wundt's inductivism but ignored his Kantian view of science. The second—and from our point of view more important—response came from Külpe and the Würzburg school, who offered a critique of Wundt's program and a new alternative.

KÜLPE

Külpe's foremost idea was that the way one perceives things depends on a predisposing attitude. If this is so, the psychological event will not depend simply on the physiology of the immediate process, but upon other psychological events as well. Perceptions, following Helmholtz's view, are learned. There are experiments which indicate the influence of predisposing attitudes; individuals will observe the repetition of the same type of event differently, depending on what they are looking for. Külpe believed that this could only be explained by predisposing ideas and 'imageless thoughts', a concept of the Würzburg school which we will discuss in more detail under that heading.

Partly on the basis of these beliefs, Külpe (who had been a student and then a follower of Wundt prior to his own experiments) broke with Wundt's program. Nevertheless, his eventual influence was similar in kind to Wundt's. He was a philosopher who aimed to devise a new theory of scientific psychology and a new approach to it. The central problem which he raised but never solved was: how can we learn when even perception depends on predisposing attitudes and imageless ideas?

Külpe was concerned to explain the psychological process by which we make judgments. The nature of this process was not clear, but was postulated to exist at an inarticulate level. Külpe thought that it could be described scientifically. To this end, he modified Wundt's method of introspection: instead of just reporting one's experience as a passive receiver, one has also to introspect or passively report the activity of judging. The Würzburg school eventually collapsed, in part because of Wundt's criticism (later pursued by Popper) that when Külpe admitted that the process was not articulate he admitted that it was not logical; and such a study had to be logical.

More importantly, the Würzburg theorists themselves did not succeed in achieving interesting experimental results beyond the original ones showing the influence of predisposing attitudes on perception. The nature of the influence proved elusive. We might also note that the existence of predisposing attitudes made the *activity* of the mind important, and yet all psychologies have passive elements. One problem lying in the background of their work, therefore, was to reconcile active and passive elements. Another problem—involving both psychology and methodology—was to explain how induction can take place.

THE WÜRZBURG SCHOOL

The work of the Würzburg school of psychologists was one of the key influences on Popper's investigations. The traditional empirical learning theory of Locke and Hume had three main features: sensationalism, associationism, and inductivism. The Würzburg school attempted to refute sensationalism, and it undermined associationism. In addition to Külpe, its guiding spirit, the major thinkers were Karl Marbe (1869–1953), Narziss Ach (1871–1942?), Henry Jackson Watt (1879–1925), and Karl Bühler.

The first breakthrough of the school was Marbe's apparent refutation of sensationalism, the doctrine that "nothing is in the mind which was not before in the senses,"[2] as Locke put it. Marbe had subjects weigh an object in each hand—the objects were close in weight—and indicate which was heavier. According to their reports of introspection, they could find no mental image or sensation which accompanied or led them to their judgment. The concept which emerged from this experiment—that of 'imageless thoughts'—stimulated the further work of the school.

Thoughts cannot be viewed purely as associations of sensations, and once one rejects the contention that ideas are pale reflections of sensation, one is forced into a theory of learning which is not purely associationist. With this in mind, Watt and Ach took a further step away from associationism. According to their theory, we have a "reproductive" tendency to associate every thought with every other thought. What presses us to adopt some associations

2. John Locke, *An Essay Concerning Human Understanding*, Book II, ch. 1.

rather than others are the tasks ["Aufgaben",] with which we are faced. Watt and Ach showed how the presentation of a particular task influences the subject's associations of a given word with another word to be produced by the subject. One interesting discovery was that with repetition the task quickly becomes unconscious, but continues to guide the associations produced.

Bühler maintained that these earlier word-association methods were too simple, and not really concerned with higher thought processes. He asked difficult, thought-provoking, yes-or-no questions, and had his subjects report their thought processes. His investigations convinced him that 'thoughts' are the fundamental elements of thinking, and that these can in no way be regarded as associations of sensations. Sensation and thought are, so to speak, two different levels. These views were openly opposed to both sensationalism and associationism.

SELZ

The problem Otto Selz attacked was: how can one explain the thinking process without appeal to either sensation or association as fundamental? In response, he produced a non-associationist theory of the thinking process. We have already discussed his definition of 'reproductive thinking' as the solving of problems by the reproduction of existing knowledge, and of 'productive thinking' as the invention of new knowledge to solve a problem. We have, as well, described his theory that the knowledge we already have and the task combine to form an incomplete structure which is the total problem, and that we complete the complex (that is, solve the problem) by closing the gap between the two.

Selz claimed that all problem solving, including productive thinking, has the nature of this completion of a complex. When an incomplete complex is presented to the mind, the mind will close the gap either by recalling the complete complex, or by creating one. He brought productive thinking into his general schema through a notion called 'means abstraction', whereby an abstraction from earlier experience is used to provide a method ('means',) of solution. He did this by forming a complex where the missing link is a 'means' to an *aim*. The incomplete complex consists of this aim, and a constraint on achievement of the aim is called a 'partial result'. Selz gives the following example: Benjamin Franklin had the aim of bringing thundercloud electricity to earth, and he knew that to do this he would have to make some connection between the cloud and the earth. The knowledge of the necessity of a connection is the partial result. The complex is completed by the idea of 'kite', which is an "abstraction, from the sight of kites flying, of the fact that they may serve as a link from earth to the cloud."[3]

Another example he gives is Michael Faraday's discovery of electromagnetic induction. The aim was to produce electricity from a magnet, and the partial result was to produce a deflection of a galvanometer needle. One day, as Faraday happened to be moving a magnet in and out of a coil with a galvanometer in the circuit, he made the means abstraction: "a *moving magnet* produces a current in a closed circuit."[4] Of course, Selz made many of his own experiments, and used such historical examples only as illustrations; but the fact that these illustrations are unrealistic history of science is not accidental.

The closing of the gap by means abstraction may be, as before, trial and error, but it will be a very narrowly directed trial and error rather than a "flight of ideas."[5] The

3. George Humphrey, *Thinking*, p. 142, quoting Selz.
4. Ibid., p. 142.
5. Otto Selz, "The Revision of the Fundamental Conceptions of Intellectual Processes", in George Mandler and Jean Matter Mandler, *Thinking*, p. 232.

closing may also be stimulated by a chance observation from which the abstraction is elicited. Selz's theory therefore is able to explain why 'chance favors the prepared mind'.

Selz's theory was an important innovation because it requires no 'associations': the knowledge of a relation is supposed to be a whole, not merely an association. Further, it has other aspects which have been taken up or rediscovered by later learning theorists. One of these is that the problem situation has a determinate structure which strongly influences the search for a solution. Another is the idea of problems as gaps in a structure. And a third is the idea of trial and error, partly but strongly constrained by the problem situation. These strong constraints led Selz to call his concept a 'theory of specific responses'. Not the least of its importance is that it was responding to a problem situation very similar to Popper's. However, as we explained earlier it also conflicts with Popper's theory at key points.

THE GESTALT SCHOOL

The Gestalt school also formed an important background to Popper's work. Its theorists were, like Selz, trying to construct a non-associationist psychology. However, they were originally concerned with a non-associationist theory of *perception*, rather than one of thinking or learning. One may take their fundamental problem to be: How can we explain the perception of independent units in the visual field other than as a constant association of atomic sense data? Their idea was to propose laws of the perception of wholes which did not rely on a specification of particular parts.[6] They achieved some success in

6. David Katz, *Gestalt Psychology*, Chap. 6.

this direction, and then tried to apply their new ideas to learning.

To understand their attempt, it is necessary to be aware of what distinguished the Gestalt psychologists as a school. We pointed out earlier that the program of the school, as personified in the work of Max Wertheiner, the founder, or of Wolfgang Köhler and Kurt Koffka, was to make over the whole of psychology into a theory of Gestalts and the laws governing them. We also noted that many psychologists contributed partial solutions to the school's basic problem of explaining the perception of individual units in a non-associationist way, but that they were not part of the school because they did not agree with all its views. Let us go into more detail in the differences.

What separated the school from Selz was mainly its view of the nature of a Gestalt. Selz regarded the knowledge of relations as wholes, and thought that the complex, a system of relations, also could be apprehended as a whole. But the Gestalt psychologists believed not only that a whole could not be reduced to the sum of its parts, but that the laws of a whole could not be fully explained even by all the parts *and their relations.* This intriguing and puzzling notion was, in their view, central to psychology.

A second, perhaps derivative, feature separated the Gestalt psychologists from the Würzburg theorists, including Bühler; this was their refusal to consider sensations at all independently of the Gestalts of which the sensations were a part. Bühler believed that thought was largely "imageless": they felt that sensation and thought had a degree of independence and that there were complex relations between the two. It was for this stand that Brunswik, as we have already stated, accused them of "structural monism." G.W. Hartmann summarizes the criticism thus: the Gestalt school "has tried to construct a mental world of form without content, making form the only ontologically real factor in experience. Instead, both the gestalt and the field-filling sensory quality must be present as correlates of the same total experience."[7]

The Gestalt theorists, like Selz, viewed learning as a problem solving activity. In order for them to carry out their program, a characteristic of learning has to be the sudden alteration of an old Gestalt or the creation of a new one, since any step by step re-association of elements is barred. Köhler called this process of alteration or creation 'insight'. Gestalt learning theory, for reasons which will appear later, was "a programme, rather than a fulfillment."[8] However, it provided two interesting beginnings to the development of learning theory.

The first, introduced by Wertheimer in 1922, is the concept of recentering to which we have already referred. Basically, the idea is that one Gestalt is changed under the pressure of a problem, and that the materials making up the Gestalt form a new one. Such is the learning process. The second idea, introduced by Koffka, is that a problem is an incomplete Gestalt, and that the solution is the "closure" of the Gestalt.

What exactly is involved in recentering? What is an incomplete Gestalt? The Gestalt theorists did not give good answers; their examples are merely illustrative. One exception is Koffka's attempt to explain how memory traces enter into the closure of a Gestalt. Koffka published his theory in 1925, and was attacked in print by both Bühler and Selz, who claimed that Koffka had lifted his theory from Selz without acknowledgement. (Selz's work had been published first in 1913 and then in 1922.) In response Koffka argued that his theory was different from Selz's, that his Gestalts were not exactly Selz's complexes, and

7. G.W. Hartmann, *Gestalt Psychology*, p. 284.
8. Humphrey, *Thinking*, p. 179.

that Selz's theory was too "mechanical" and did not entirely escape the spirit of associationism. Nevertheless, at the level of specific examples the explanation can as easily be made in terms of incomplete complexes as of incomplete Gestalts. Koffka did not really succeed in showing that his theory could do more than could Selz's. The conflict indicates the weakness of both theories.

In order to understand Popper's relation to these developments, some chronology is necessary. The Würzburg school was active in the early years of the nineteenth century, with Bühler's culminating paper appearing in 1907. The work of the school continued after this, but its basic positions were not altered. Wertheimer's first Gestalt paper was written in 1912; Köhler's book *The Mentality of Apes* appeared in 1917; Wertheimer's essay on "The Closure Process in Productive Thinking" appeared in 1920. Koffka's work on the subject was published during the twenties; his book *The Growth of the Mind* came out in 1925. Popper was aware of some of the Gestalt thinking, but apparently he did not know the work of the Würzburg school until he met Bühler in 1925. He had completed his own psychological work before he learned of Selz.[9]

Like Selz and the Gestalt psychologists, Popper was interested in the problem of explaining learning by a non-associationist theory and especially interested in developing a non-associationist theory of the creative thought processes. This is not surprising, given the history of psychology in the preceding years. It was not even necessary that he be familiar with the details of the history; the Gestalt psychologists were openly anti-associationist, and no well worked out non-associationist theory of creative problem solving had been produced.

9. Karl Popper, "Autobiography of Karl Popper", *The Philosophy of Karl Popper*, ed. Paul Arthur Schilpp, p. 60.

BÜHLER

Karl Bühler was a leading student of Külpe. The Würzburg school, of which Bühler was a member, ceased to be active after the early thirties, but it had notable offspring. Popper is in effect one of its children. Though he had independent influences, he learned from and reacted to the Würzburg school. Some of its influences on him can be identified fairly clearly, and Bühler was one of the greatest.

Bühler is important for us here because he attempted to develop and carry through Külpe's program, because this attempt at development uncovered the difficulties in the school, and because he was Popper's teacher. Popper's Ph.D. dissertation defends Bühler's approach to psychology, and Popper's views were developed in the intellectual milieu provided by Bühler and became clearly defined by Bühler's influence and Popper's reaction to him.

Bühler's own intellectual concerns grew out of Külpe's program. Like Külpe, Bühler believed the central problem of the psychology of thinking to be how we make judgments. Furthermore, he agreed with Külpe that our intellectual conceptions and our immediate perceptions lie along a continuum yet can, to a degree, be distinguished.[10] Our intellectual conceptions influence our immediate perceptions, and our perceptual experience has been a formative influence on our intellectual conceptions. Yet our conceptions have not arisen from the reception of sense information alone; our intellect actively constructs ideas which it uses to interpret sense experience.

When we recall that Külpe also accepted Helmholtz's idea that perception is (partly) learned, we can see the distinctive character of Külpe's view of the mind. Though perception is partly learned, as Helmholtz believed, it is *not* learned by the association of elements of earlier sen-

10. Karl Bühler, *The Mental Development of the Child*, p. 85–86.

sations. And though perception is influenced by physiology, as Wundt proposed, it is also influenced by the partly independent products of the active intellect. According to Külpe, then, the intellect actively constructs ideas which can change and develop and which in turn influence our perception and our thinking at every level. This distinctive approach, we should note, is the starting point not only of Bühler's work, but also of that of the rest of the Würzburg school, of the Gestalt school (which also had personal contact with Külpe), and of Popper. Külpe's viewpoint is the fountainhead of a great deal of important work in psychology and philosophy in the twentieth century.

Bühler especially wanted to find out how our ideas are developed on the highest level of the intellect; he sought laws of the functioning of these highest mental processes. In his early experiments, as we mentioned before, he had attempted to use methods of introspection to study these processes, methods that were attacked by Wundt as unreliable and unscientific. From those early experiments, Bühler concluded that the 'thoughts' involved in coming to an answer cannot be considered as images or as derived from images.

Bühler then turned to language for a clue to understanding the development of our ideas. He was able to distinguish three levels of language. The lowest is the indicative or expressive level; an example of it is the instinctive cry when one suddenly steps on a sharp object. The next level is the release or signalling function; here the cry influences the actions of another person or animal. The highest level is descriptive. The levels are ascending in that the lower levels may be present without the higher levels, but not *vice versa*.

He was able to apply the idea of levels to child psychology as well, where he distinguished levels of instinct, training, and intellect. No doubt he was searching for the laws of the development and interaction of these levels, but he was not able to carry his ideas very far in that direction. Although he was unable to work out any detailed theory of the development of conceptions, he clearly rejected the idea that they can be learned by the repetition of specific instances, as Hume thought.[11] However, he was willing to admit that induction as a means of justification is permissible.

One issue in which Bühler's influence on Popper is clear involves Bühler's methods of research. Both Külpe and Bühler had a serious methodological problem. If perception involves active interpretation in the light of previously learned ideas, introspection would be expected to involve interpretation as well as the reporting of bare facts. Where such interpretation is involved, it may introduce errors. How can evidence acquired in this way be used profitably? The problem was most acute for Bühler because his method involved introspective reporting on the most complex thought processes. As we have mentioned, Wundt claimed that this method was illegitimate for psychology. In his Ph.D. thesis, Popper defended Bühler's methods of research. Appealing to Bühler's three levels of language, he argued that in order to study them we need to use all major methods of approach to experimental psychology—the behavioral, the experiential or introspective, and the description of "objective mental structures" (the study of the actual sentences produced is one kind of objective mental structure). Only thus, he contended, will we be able to provide a theory which does justice to a further aspect of psychology, the biological and evolutionary aspects of man.[12]

Popper also referred to J.F. Fries' criticism of Kant's approach. Fries (1773–1843) had argued that in justifying knowledge we are led either to infinite regress, to dogma-

---

11. Ibid., pp. 151–153.
12. Karl Popper, "Zur Methodenfrage der Denkpsychologie," Ph.D. dissertation University of Vienna, 1928.

tism, or to psychologism. Fries preferred psychologism. Popper was later to present a new solution to Fries' 'trilemma'.

Though he provided new arguments for the legitimacy of Bühler's approach, Popper had not really grappled with the fundamental problems of the validity of the introspective method. He was not satisfied with his efforts, but he did not attempt to improve on them. Instead, he soon focused his attention on the problems of the methodology of the physical sciences.

Popper may have been influenced as well by Bühler's rejection of Hume's theory of induction; or, more precisely, of Kant's reading of Hume's theory, according to which repetition of specific experiences causes general theories to arise in the mind. Popper had independent reasons for attacking Hume's theory, so it is not clear how much was Bühler's influence and how much coincidence of aims. Popper's psychology was also more thoroughly anti-inductivist than was Bühler's. For Bühler, though no perception is free of the influence of thought, the progress of knowledge occurs through the gradual clarification and fixing of ideas, a process which is supposed to ascend from the more perceptual to the more conceptual end of the spectrum. For Popper, clear and fairly rigid theories are to be formed on the higher levels of generality, but then modified in the light of counter-examples.

Perhaps more influential than Bühler's rejection of psychological induction was his simultaneous acceptance of induction as a process of justification. In this clear divergence, Popper saw the need for an alternative to induction on the level of the evaluation of theories. Another influence by reaction concerned Külpe's and Bühler's attitude toward logic. They felt that logic can be regarded as a theory of judgments. Popper, following recent trends in logic, thought it was necessary to clearly separate logic and psychology.

115

Bühler probably was most influential as a transmitter of Külpe's basic view of the mind. The idea that the mind actively creates general theories which grow, change, and influence further thought and perception at every level is the basic presupposition from which Popper developed all his psychological and methodological theories.

6
FALLIBILISM VERSUS STIMULUS-RESPONSE THEORY

THE REDUCTIONIST PROGRAM IN PSYCHOLOGY

In our analysis so far, we have mostly concentrated on the history of psychology in the German-speaking world. Yet, according to the most widely accepted interpretation of the history of scientific psychology, the major success story of the late nineteenth and early twentieth century psychology of learning is not the German tradition: it is stimulus-response psychology, and mainly that practised in America. It is such thinkers as Edward Lee Thorndike (1874–1949), Ivan P. Pavlov (1849–1936), John Broadus Watson (1878–1958), Edward Chace Tolman (1886–1959), Clark Leonard Hull (1884–1952), B.F. Skinner, Neal Elgan Miller, and W.K. Estes who are deemed the most successful learning theorists by the community of psychologists.

Some thinkers working within the tradition of stimulus-response psychology, such as Tolman, have proposed Gestalt learning theories using concepts of whole, of fields or space, or of purpose. In our view, all these theories fail for the same fundamental reasons that those of the more immediate followers of Külpe did: they attempt to form a learning theory using a methodology which presumes that science will achieve the full and certain truth, and they attempt to explain psychologically how this truth will be obtained. They also fail because they retain associationist principles. It is not immediately apparent that these psychologists succumbed to the same difficulties as the Külpe school, especially since the standard view is that they succeeded where others failed. This view is misleading.

The Külpe school (or schools) openly tried to develop psychological theories using a non-reductionist technique. When their experiments showed that reduction of psychological states (perceptions, thoughts, and feelings) to rudimentary elements is not feasible, they tried to construct a theory using new concepts and views of the mind. This led to difficulties in explaining how some perception, thought, or feeling not reducible to elements can be judged to be true. They retained inductivist views developed in conjunction with associationism.

The stimulus-response theorists, on the other hand, all maintained reductionist views. Some simply ignored the new problems; others attempted to explain them away. They seemed to have a program both for pursuing psychology (reductionism) and for their psychological theory (the stimulus-response theory) which could explain how both ordinary learning and psychological research can lead to the truth, even if concepts such as purpose or Gestalt are needed.

The central tenet of their program is that if theories or

concepts are *reduced to known elements* they may be scientific; that is, known either with certainty or something approaching certainty. The main problem is to carry out this reduction. The reduction itself serves as confirmation of the theory reduced. We wish to criticize this view; we will do so by explaining how the methodological, metaphysical, and psychological theories all pursue the aim of reduction but that attempts to carry through the program—and thereby explain away the new discoveries of the Külpe school—lead to untestable theories and narrow observation. We believe this failure to be due to the difficulty plaguing simultaneously the methodology and the psychology; that is, that all 'elements' are theory-dependent.

The rationale for the reductionist program has methodological, metaphysical, and psychological sources. The methodological reason for pursuing reduction is that science is, and ought to be, only about observations. If we go beyond observations, we will lapse into speculation, error, and perhaps even meaningless nonsense. Various methodologies—the inductivism and/or conventionalism of the Vienna Circle and the conventionalist operationalism of P.W. Bridgman (1882–1961)—endorse the reductionist program. They have differences, of course, but the common reductionist aim is far more important.

The metaphysical reason for pursuing a reductionist program arises from the defence of behaviorism. Psychologists do not commonly consider behaviorism to be a metaphysics; it is supposed to be a non-metaphysical approach which can remove the need for a metaphysics. Thus behaviorism, just as the prevailing methodologies, appears to offer a way of eliminating metaphysics. The programs are identical. The behaviorist anti-metaphysics is also reductionist. It is thought that if all descriptions of human action are descriptive of behavior, metaphysics will be eliminated. This claim is untenable because the theory that human action is explainable by a particular kind of event is a metaphysics itself.

The third rationale for the reductionist program lies in the prevailing associationist psychology. According to this doctrine, the mind obeys laws which describe how elements are related, combined, separated, and so on. Traditionally, these elements were perceptions, thoughts, or feelings identified by introspection. When this reductionist program failed, the program of the reduction of psychological description to statements about behavior succeeded it. It was proposed that major tenets of associationism can be saved if, instead of seeking laws of the association of mental elements, we seek laws of the association of *external* elements; that is, of bits of behavior.

The overwhelming influence of the many variants of stimulus-response (reflex) psychology can be explained by the fact that these psychologies provide a definite program for the reduction of psychological terms to elements and the laws connecting them. This is why the various sources of stimulus-response psychology are obscured. The same program is used to implement the scientific study of psychology, to eliminate metaphysics, and to develop a variant of associationist psychology.

CRITIQUE OF THE REDUCTIONIST PROGRAM

The three major objections to the reductionist program are metaphysical, methodological, and psychological. As we have already pointed out, the now widely accepted criticism of the anti-metaphysical program is that it is itself a metaphysics. If metaphysical theories are theories of what the world is made of, a theory that the world is made of facts or sensations or matter alone is also a metaphysics. This simple and powerful criticism has not had a great deal of impact on psychologists, probably due to the widespread belief that whether the behaviorist program theory is metaphysical or not, science requires it for methodological reasons.

The foundation of the methodological grounds for a reductionist program is the quest for certainty. Psychologists have accepted both the view that scientific results should be certain or near-certain and that psychologists have not in general reached this goal. Therefore they wish to apply the principles of scientific method with even more vigor than do physical scientists. They interpret these principles as forbidding speculation, so they attempt to find ways of preventing any speculative elements from entering theories. There are two standard means of accomplishing this end: to state all terms in operational definitions, and to confirm theories.

These two means have originated from two profoundly different philosophies of science which merge in psychology. The first—to state all terms in operational definitions—is a development of a conventionalist philosophy of science. This view argues that the hope of discovering the nature of reality must be abandoned; that there is no way of guaranteeing the truth of any theory. Faced with this failure to justify induction, it is proposed that if science lowers its aims by seeking only true predictions it can achieve certainty. Though we will never know the nature of reality, we will be able to control the world; we will be able to make true predictions.

The second means—to confirm theories—is simply a corollary of the inductivist view of science. True statements about the nature of reality can be known with certainty or near certainty if they are (properly) confirmed. The difficulty that psychologists face in attempting to use this theory is that what counts as a proper confirmation is not adequately explained by any inductivist: any reasonably interesting highly confirmed theory—even Newton's—still may turn out to be false.

As a result, both operationalism and inductivism are interpreted in very narrow ways: we should say as little as possible, so that we may be as certain as possible. If we can explain what our theories mean empirically, then this goal will be achieved. Thus the two tend to be conflated, and the claims that psychologists make for their theories are often muddled: are their views true or only useful?[1]

Thus the reductionist program becomes a corollary of both inductivism and conventionalism when applied to psychology. Both presume that certainty of some sort can be achieved, but the attempt to do so leads to the paradoxical result that no interesting empirical claim is permitted—all claims are trivial. Yet the broad metaphysical theses about reduction and method are taken as obvious. The triviality is due to the logical impossibility of reducing universal theories to a finite series of singular observation statements. The attempt to reduce theory to observation in fact drains theory of empirical content. The singular statements are (wrongly) presumed to be certain, the theories which go beyond them conjectural. For the sake of reliability, an attempt is made to stay with the lowest level. The result is a series of examples, a vague interpretative program, and little in between. This situation tends to force any interesting discussion out of psychology.

The final objection to the reductionist program is the psychological one. If psychologists seek (certain) psychological laws of the association of (mental, behavioral, and psychological) entities, they must be able to identify these elements. This identification is a primary aim of the reductionist program. However, in order to have the program it is necessary to have a conception of ele-

1. This confusion came to the surface in the famous Tolman-Hull debate over intervening variables. The theory that intervening variables need to be specified is a theory that operationalism is not sufficient.

mental entities. Traditional associationist psychology—which says that psychological laws are laws of the association of mental entities—has collapsed. The only associationist alternative, stimulus-response theory—which holds that psychological laws are laws of the association of stimuli and responses—obviously must be accepted. However, this reductionist rationale for stimulus-response will not work. The criticism made of traditional associationism applies to it, as well. We cannot, either as normal subjects of study or as scientist-observers, identify stimuli or generate responses without using predisposing attitudes that are not reducible to sensation. The powerful conclusion of perception theory is that stimuli cannot be identified independently of a framework. Any psychology which fails to account for the framework is inadequate.

Again, the nonexistence of psychological induction deals a death blow to the stimulus-response approach. As individuals, we use general theories which go beyond particular observation and are not derivable from particular observations. For example, we have theories about what is going to happen in the future, and these theories affect our purposes and our view of the present situation. Thus our purposes and conceptions cannot be reduced to a sum of previous particular stimuli and responses, nor can our behavior be explained on that basis. Moreover, as psychologists observing others, we are going beyond observation in isolating some features of a situation as stimuli and others as responses; this selection of singular facts is influenced by theories, whether or not we are conscious of them.

These failings of the stimulus-response belief point up the fact that the learning theories of stimulus-response and the Külpe school failed for a near-identical reason: neither accounted for the breakdown of associationism in their *method* of carrying out psychology.

THE CASE OF TOLMAN

In our view, for a non-associationist learning theory to be successful, it must also be non-reductionist. Therefore, we have not dealt so far with non-associationist variants of learning theory that seek to vindicate a reductionist approach. These variants nevertheless exist: psychologists such as E.C. Tolman have attempted to show that concepts which are not *prima facie* allowable in the stimulus response program and which have importance for Külpe and his school can be rendered acceptable by a reductionist program. Their problem is caused by the perceived need, resulting from the research of Külpe and those whom he influenced most heavily, to use concepts of purpose and of predisposing tendencies, and/or of concepts of wholes not (yet) reducible to elements.

The difficulties of developing a psychological theory which incorporates the significant results of the Külpe school only appear to be avoided. The myth that they are avoided is one of the greatest blocks to solving the problems which the theory raises. We will use Tolman's work to illustrate both the failure to resolve these difficulties and, in fact, the bankruptcy of reductionist psychology.

Basically, Tolman attempts to render such concepts as purpose and cognition empirical by reduction to observable events, thereby removing the need for special theories of these attributes which require the study of something other than observed events. Indeed, the central problem for such theories is to study empirically the activities of the mind. We argue that his attempt to explain this problem away fails to achieve the empirical theories of purpose or cognition which it seeks: it only supplies, in a new language, descriptions of particular bits of behavior which fail to explain and to be extended to other areas; that is, to be independently testable.

The failure is common to other attempts as well, but is

of particular interest here because it is precisely the problem of the creation of empirical theories of cognition that was so acute for non-associationist psychologists. It may be useful to point out that methods of reduction fail to solve the problem for either associationist or non-associationist concepts. Or, let us say, the reduction of non-associationist to associationist concepts fails to generate the desired empirical theories, as the use of associationist-reductionist concepts alone has also failed. Instead we have the original metaphysical theory and narrow descriptions of specific bits of behavior.

In his book *Purposive Behavior in Animals and Men*, Tolman proposes that we eliminate from psychology any reference to mentalistic or dualistic entities. He wants to define terms which in the past have been interpreted dualistically or mentalistically, without the assumption of mentalistic entities. He claims that doing so will further the formation of a scientific and predictive psychology. The concepts of 'purpose' and 'motivation', he believes, are needed to describe behavior, but should be made legitimate by defining them in terms of observable features. In his view, a term will be acceptable if specifiable, observable processes are its definition. In order to construct such definitions, he analyzes some of the situations in which such terms are used or needed and specifies the different observable characteristics of such events. In doing so he forms a system for the cataloguing or description of mental events, a system which consists of the definitions of the various terms needed for reference to mental events. He states, ". . . the perusal of this glossary may even serve as a convenient way of reviewing and summarizing the entire doctrine."[2]

Central to Tolman's theory is his notion of 'intervening variables'. It can most easily be explained by example. The

2. E.C. Tolman, *Purposive Behavior in Animals and Men*, p. xi.

125

sight of food is a stimulus to which animals respond by moving toward the food and eating it. The movement only occurs if there is sight of the food and the purpose to eat. The purpose or cognition in a situation thus become variables in the description or explanation of the event. Tolman wants to avoid the view by which terms refer to unobserved mentalistic entities which operate between stimulus and response: instead, he wishes to define these variables in terms of the observed behavior of the animal. The terms or processes so defined are called intervening variables.

The interpretation provided here suggests that Tolman has a metapsychological theory of behavior which contends that animals have purposes which control their actions. However, the purposes can only be defined by the learning behavior. Tolman argues that learning can take place independent of rewards of purposes; that it is cognitive in the sense that response is to signs or patterns of sign-Gestalts. Animals, he contends, do not learn to respond simply to stimuli, but to stimuli as signs of something else which are perceived by forming Gestalt patterns of perception. He summarizes his work as follows:

> Our system has been presented. It conceives mental processes as functional variables intervening between stimuli, initiating psychological states and the general heredity and past training of the organism, on the one hand, and final resulting responses, on the other, these intervening variables it defines as behavior determinants. And these behavior determinants it subdivides further into (1) immanent purposive and cognitive determinants, (2) capacities, (3) behavior-adjustments. All three of these types of determinants are to be discovered, in the last analysis, by behavior experiments. They have to be inferred "back" from behavior. They are precipitated out from the empirical correlations which can be observed between specific

126

stimuli and initiating psychological states on the one hand, and specific resultant acts on the other. They are to behavior as electrons, waves, or whatever it may be are to happenings in organic matter. There is nothing private or "mentalistic" about them. They are pragmatically conceived objective variables, the concepts of which can be altered and changed as proves most useful.[3]

We will turn now to two examples of hypotheses which are part of Tolman's metapsychological theory, which are not refutable, and which are used as research programs (though quite limited ones) in the formation of narrow auxiliary theories which fail to be independently testable.[4] Our two examples concern what Tolman calls behavior determinants and, more precisely, immanent purposive and cognitive determinants. The two determinants are "demand for a goal object" and "discriminandum."

Tolman claims that in experiments in which rats run a maze there is a need for distinguishing an observable aspect of the situation—that is, a "demand for":

> It appears that, given one and the same physiological drive, certain goal-objects, when provided at the end of the maze, produce more efficient maze-performance than do others. And this lends us to the assumption

---

3. Ibid., p. 414.

4. Tolman contends that experiments can provide support for his system. "The evidence (for my system) such as it is, I find throughout all the experiments on instrumental learning, wherever done. At least I am almost always capable of translating, or if you will, distorting, this evidence so as to use it as support for my system." And he also states that his studies are exceedingly narrow: "I have always wanted my psychology to be as wide as the study of a life career and as narrow as the study of a rat's entrance into a specific blind. But, actually, I have for the most part studied only average numbers of entrances into specific blinds, or jumps to a particular type of door, and have hoped that the principles found there would have something to do with a really interesting piece of behavior— say the choice and pursuit of a life career." E.C. Tolman, *Principles of Purposive Behavior*, n.p.

of a variable to be designated the 'demand for the goal-object.'[5]

The concept of 'demand for the goal-object' is, according to Tolman, made necessary because rats run mazes differently when different rewards are presented. The substitution of "poor" goal-objects for "good" ones will produce a reduction in the facility with which the maze is run, and the opposite substitution will, of course, produce an increase.

> To sum up: the three experiments just cited all indicate that, given one and the same hunger condition, different groups of rats, provided with different types of food or food-situation at the goal-box, will exhibit different apparent rates of learning and different degrees of final performance. And this, we say, defines an immanent determinant of maze performance which we may designate as the demand for certain types of goal-object (given a particular drive).[6]

"Demand for" is thus defined experimentally or observationally as being the rate or comparative rates at which rats run mazes or pursue ends when there are different goals. The "demand for" may be observed and measured.

The theory that there is a cause of behavior which is a "demand for" cannot be refuted: it is already shown to exist by the presentation of the theory. Furthermore, the theory makes no predictions about particular instances of "demand for." If we should fail to find it—i.e. if there were no difference between the rates at which rats run mazes or some other pursuit of goals—Tolman would conclude that the "demand for" factor is equal. The theory thus provides a program for describing events but is not itself predictive of any events. It incorporates the concept only by prevent-

5. Tolman, *Purposive Behavior*, p. 67.
6. Ibid., p. 46.

ing its use in any explanation and by preventing any explanation of the factor itself.

However, Tolman's theory can be used as a research program for the formation of auxiliary hypotheses. The theory states that there is a particular factor which functions as a cause of behavior. The research program is to discover the functioning of this factor in various instances. Tolman, for example, found that the "demand for" of rats for bran mash is greater than that for sunflower seed.[7] This theory, of course, is predictive: it predicts that rats will learn to run mazes faster when the reward is bran mash than when it is sunflower seed. But this is the event it is designed to explain. It makes no new predictions. It fails to be independently testable. It is true that we can multiply such narrow theories, but multiplication only gives us a great number of auxiliary theories which fail to be independently testable. And independent tests are necessary if psychology is to progress in the way that the physical sciences have progressed.

Let us now turn to the second determinant, "discriminandum". According to Tolman, any animal has "expectations": this can be seen by observing that certain signs or stimuli will lead to the continuation of certain forms of behavior and certain others will lead to discontinuation. For example, a rat may expect a certain reward at the end of a maze—say, water. If the rat is thirsty, he will run the maze more quickly than if he is hungry: he "expects" water to be at the end of the maze.[8] "Discriminanda" are the signs which lead an animal or man to expect certain results. They are behavior supports, required for the carrying through of certain sorts of behavior. The metapsychological hypothesis, then, is that there are "discriminanda" which function in determining behavior.

7. Ibid., pp. 45–46.
8. Ibid., pp. 71–72.

Again, this hypothesis is irrefutable: it has already been shown by definition that "discriminanda" exist. What is left is to discover what particular discriminanda operate in particular situations. For example, in some experiments it was found that changes in odors in the maze affect behavior.[9] The listing of the discriminanda and the explanation of their relation to specific sorts of behavior becomes the job of the psychologist. It is again evident that this is a research program that can generate narrow auxiliary theories about particular rats in particular mazes. It may also generate theories about the ability of a rat or other organism to distinguish various sorts of sensations. But these theories all fail to be independently testable. They do no more than describe various sorts of experiments which are done. For instance, they might predict that a particular organism can distinguish sounds of a certain pitch from sounds a degree different, but we could only test such a theory by repeated attempts to get the organism to make a finer distinction. Tolman advocates using his theory as a research tool to form those sorts of theories:

> . . . an expected discriminandum is to be defined by the range of sense-characters, any one of which may be substituted in the given situation and support the discrimination behavior in question equally well. But further, this empirically determined range of such satisfactory or supporting environmental characters must in its turn be defined not in simple physical terms, but rather in terms of that whole system or intrinsic order of differentiabilities, which is found to obtain relative to this class of sensory characters for this type of organism. In other words, by means of purely objective discrimination experiments, there is to be worked out for every type of organism sense-polyhedrons (analogous to the color-pyramid for human beings) in each sense mode of the given organ-

9. Ibid., p. 79.

130

ism. And an expected discriminandum is always to be defined, in the last analysis, with reference to such a polyhedron or "intrinsic order" of differentiabilities.[10]

To recapitulate, then, the theories that animals have a purposive and a cognitive determinant are not testable because they do not provide a way of determining whether animals have such mental or behavioral characteristics, other than by observing phenomena and describing them in terms of the determinants. It has been shown possible to do this: if we fail, however, we conclude that the factor is not effective or not present in a particular situation.

Tolman's general theory makes no prediction about the functioning of particular instances of "demand for" and "discriminandum,"[11] and thus serves no role in generating explanations. It fails even to allow for explanations of these factors or how they function. It does provide a method for generating narrow auxiliary theories, but any particular description of behavior does not follow from Tolman's system. His experimental definitions of concepts employ his metapsychological theory as a methodological one. For instance, we may determine the amount of "demand for" which a rat has for a particular type of food a certain time after last feeding, or what signs in what patterns can be learned by rats in running a maze. Again, both these sorts of theories are not independently testable. They do not generate new tests, but only allow for repeated testing of the rat in the maze in a particular situation. They are simply auxiliary theories which enable Tol-

---

10. Ibid., p. 88.

11. E.R. Guthrie says: "Signs, in Tolman's theory, occasion in the rat *realization*, or *cognition*, or *judgment*, or *hypotheses*, or *abstraction*, but they do not occasion action. In his concern with what goes on in the rat's mind, Tolman has neglected to predict what the rat will do. So far as the theory is concerned the rat is left buried in thought; if it gets to the food box at the end that is its concern, not the concern of the theory." E.R. Guthrie, *The Psychology of Learning*, p. 144.

man to interpret events in terms of the metapsychological theory.

We must conclude that attempts to use Gestalt concepts in a reductionist program fail to achieve the aims of explanation, confirmation, or predictive power. They do not enable us to explain either purpose or cognition, and they fail to say anything interesting about these important psychological factors. These failures are direct consequences of the use of a reductionist program. Not only does the program fail, theorists who use it are blocked from developing explanations.

7
THE CURRENT PROBLEM
SITUATION

According to the prevailing view, the nineteenth century brought the rise of scientific psychology. Histories of late nineteenth and early twentieth century psychology and philosophy relate the story of the thought of this period in two strands, one psychological and the other philosophical.[1] In this account we have shown that there is a continuous interaction of the two. Clearly there is a tension between the myth of the rise of an independent scientific

1. For a critical discussion of such histories, see John Wettersten, "The Historiography of Scientific Psychology: A Critical Study", *Journal of the History of the Behavioural Sciences*, (April 1975): 157–171. Also see Wettersten, "The Philosophy of Science and the History of Science: Separate Aspects vs. Separate Domains", *Philosophical Forum*, forthcoming.

psychology and the reality of the strong interaction of psychological and philosophical theories. We wish to conclude our essay by beginning to redress this error. It should be rectified not only in order to improve our histories, but also because this historical myth serves as a restricting and unrealistic framework for current research.

Nineteenth century German philosopher-psychologists did indeed attempt, in reaction to Kant, to form theories of scientific psychology. The major result, however, was not a separate scientific psychology but the formation of philosophical theories of scientific psychology which interacted with psychological research and which, contrary to the myth, continue to this day to affect both fields. The misinterpretation of this research has led to confusion on both sides of the alleged divide between psychology and philosophy as well as to confusion about the history of each.

A central thesis of our account is that much research in psychology could have taken a more productive path. We contend that some psychology of the 1930s is more up-to-date than most contemporary stimulus-response psychology. There are neglected problems of non-associationist learning theory which we will discuss, and which offer a more interesting and fruitful line of research than do current stimulus-response theories. We have seen from the work of Külpe and his followers that even perception depends on thought. Furthermore, thoughts or predisposing ideas are neither justified nor veridical; they are conjectural and thus not dependable. In fact, there is no epistemologically dependable psychological state. Yet all contemporary learning theory behaves as if there were. Nonassociationists seek some dependable state; associationists presume that the state exists and seek the rules of its use. Physiological psychology either ignores the problem—when the physiology is to the fore—or accepts the concept of a dependable state—when, for example, physiology is the foundation of a theory of how knowledge is possible, as proposed by Donald Hebb.

We are left with a paradoxical situation, wherein a crucial conclusion of nineteenth and twentieth century psychology and philosophy—that all psychological states are influenced by conjecture—is often ignored in methodology and psychology. All of the dominant traditions in psychology and methodology pose problems in frameworks which ignore this discovery. As a result, the 'up-to-date' work is out-of-date.

THE SEGREGATION OF PSYCHOLOGY
AND METHODOLOGY

In our view, the obstacle to advance in psychology and methodology is the segregation of the two. Both have attempted to advance separately. Both have endorsed the segregation as necessary to maintain the scientific state of psychology and to give methodology a definite, stable, and independent subject matter to study. This segregation, however, cannot be maintained. Theorists on each side of the divide accept results from the other side as given. Psychologists presume knowledge of scientific method as a background to their research. Methodologists accept and make use of some assumptions from psychology.

This implicit recognition poses problems, of course, since neither group is unified. Psychologists may choose varying methodologies, and do; methodologists may choose varying psychologies, and do. However, the manner of this choice makes interaction limited. A member of one group may choose any view of the other but is limited to those views endorsed by some appropriate community. Furthermore, his acceptance must be largely uncritical. If he wishes to transform the other discipline to fit his own demands or problems, he breaks the barrier, and in doing so destroys the integrity of his own discipline. The integrity of each depends on segregation from the other.

The attempt at segregation did double harm in Popper's work. Because they conflicted with the (non-psychological) methodological framework of the psychologists, new proposals in psychology could not be brought forward. Learning by replacement of theories could not be considered as learning, nor could the growth of Popper's methodology out of his new psychology be presented.

This failure in both the presentation and the understanding of Popper's views brought the study of psychology and methodology to a standstill. The only solution to the predicament facing both disciplines could not be presented. The psychology was hidden entirely. The new psychological assumption of the methodology proved a powerful obstacle in the way of acceptance by methodologists because, if they were to be considered "serious", they had to accept the views of established psychology. Neither field could break out of its narrow bounds because each would have had to change the other in order to do so. Popper did break out, of course, and we believe that the cool reception he received is due to the deeper problems his break raises. One of these is the theory of the independence of scientific psychology from methodology.

THREE ASSOCIATIONIST BLOCKS
IN CONTEMPORARY PSYCHOLOGY
AND METHODOLOGY

It is generally conceded that introspection has failed as a method of undertaking scientific psychology. First, the elements of introspection proved to be elusive; experiments showing the influence of predisposing attitudes were eventually decisive. Secondly, even those psychologists who did not accept this criticism failed to generate laws of association. This failure tended to corroborate the basic tenet of the first criticism; that is, that there are no discrete elements of thought knowable by introspection.

Crucial to the collapse, however, was an alternative—the stimulus-response psychology of Thorndike, Pavlov, and Watson. Stimulus-response psychology fell on fertile ground because it seemed to resolve the difficulties in introspection psychology by identifying elements which could then be associated in accord with laws. In following this approach, psychology could maintain associationism simply by making elements external rather than internal. Inductivism could also be saved, since the psychology of stimulus-response provided a psychological basis for inductivism.

Stimulus-response psychology has a bad conscience, however, because if it is to proceed it needs a theory of the identification of the elements, i.e. of stimuli and responses. If the content of ideas and perceptions depends on predisposing ideas, then the identification of stimuli and responses, either by actor or observer (i.e. psychologist), also depends on such predisposing ideas. Yet the stimulus-response program depends on the objective identification of stimulus and response. Both psychologist and experimental subject must perceive stimulus and response in the same way and do so independently. Thus the stimulus-response program simply hides, rather than coming to terms with, the main problem which led to the collapse of introspective psychology.

Psychologists have been aware of this difficulty but rarely have formulated it clearly. We conjecture that this is because the criticism is effective against all versions of associationism, and yet some version of associationism is crucial to most "scientific" psychology.

Conventionalism appeared to be a way out of the dilemma of associationism, since it could enable psychologists to specify with operations the terms which were apparently irreducible. Tolman's essay "Purposive Behavior in Animals and Men," is the classic attempt to carry through this program. Ironically, the criticism of associationism—which shows that the reduction of theory to fundamental, independent, observed operations is impossible because the observed operations themselves need to be specified with theory—is also a refutation of conventionalism. Yet, even though psychologists have at hand a refutation of the methodological theory they have attempted to employ, they continue to use the theory. Presumably they do so because methodology—especially methodology endorsed by physicists—is an independent discipline.

There is further irony here. The reductionist concepts employed by psychologists maintain the view—now outdated in philosophy—that knowledge can grow by accumulating facts or low-level hypotheses and then building upon them in ever broader generalizations. But it was recognized by psychologists that this theory depended on knowledge of discrete facts. They had a bad conscience about this, and for good reason: associationism collapsed because of its failure to find such facts. The resulting method is a curious combination of a conventionalist view of facts or low-level hypotheses and an inductivist view of the growth of knowledge.[2] But its influence is widespread.

A second major claim of stimulus-response psychology has been that it has successfully formulated psychological laws. This claim cannot be true if the elements it presumes to exist in fact do not. No feasible laws can exist if the elements are ephemeral or identified in *ad hoc* ways. In fact, they do not exist. An easy method of confirmation is almost universally used in scientific psychology to show the existence of such laws. The basic technique is to make a prediction and, if it comes out badly, to modify the

2. This is found most clearly in Burrhus F. Skinner, *Science and Human Behavior.*

138

theory in some *ad hoc* way. Classic examples are Pavlov's theory of sleep as inhibition and Hull's theory of negative reinforcement. A second and more widely used technique—that of such theorists as Hull, Skinner, Hebb, and Estes—is not to predict at all but simply to count successful interpretations as confirmations of the theories used to interpret.

The story of the most significant block, the failure of nonassociationist learning theory, is not, of course, one of complete failure: advances were made in spite of it. The program was continued by Edgar Rubin (1886–1951), Adriaan de Groot, David Katz, and others: nevertheless, with the exception of Piaget's work, it was eclipsed. The break begins with Külpe, whose experiments indicated that perception depends on predisposing ideas. He saw, too, that all existing programs of scientific psychology would have to be reconsidered, and he attempted to develop an alternative.

His break from associationist psychology was radical. He rejected the foundation of all associationist views—the existence of elements of perception. Yet his attempt to reformulate the program of scientific psychology was conservative: it retained an introspective and inductivist method. His method of introspection presumed the passive observation of an active mind, a result of his implicit acceptance of inductivist—therefore passivist—methodology when his psychology took the contrary view.

The depth of the conflict is only apparent, however, when we look at Külpe's followers—the Würzburg thinkers, Selz, the Gestalt psychologists, and Piaget. As we explained earlier, all these theorists continued to develop Külpe's thesis that thought is not derived from sensation. This negative thesis posed a new problem: how is knowledge possible if it is not so derived, nor a product of an innate and anterior framework? This may appear to be a methodological problem. It is. But it was also the central problem of Külpe's followers. They assumed that learning meant learning the truth, and that therefore they had to provide a psychological explanation of how truth was obtained, even though they had already rejected the psychology which undergirded the methodology which was the source of the demand.

Though the various learning theories broke down on this point, there was some success: the Gestalt psychologists initiated the study of insight, and Piaget instituted the study of thought structure and logic. These successes, however, are only partial, because they presuppose that the learner acquires a final rigid structure which is also true. This view is methodologically untenable. We believe it is also psychologically untenable because, in order to maintain it, one has to reconcile a view of the mind as a passive receptacle of unquestioned objects of perception or thought with a view of the mind as actively constructing such elements—which are, with the rejection of Kant's doctrine of *a priori* forms, questionable.

The pursuit of a non-associationist learning theory, then, was blocked by the failure to develop either a theory which explains how truth is attained or one which explains how knowledge is possible without truth. Popper removed this obstacle, but his achievement has been obscured because he continued to segregate psychology and methodology and to bury his own psychology.

Popper himself did not develop a theory of the use of fallible introspection in psychological research; in fact, formation of such a theory was probably inhibited by the overly stringent standards which we discussed in Chapter 3. However, as we have noted, Joseph Agassi's theory of evidence along Popperian lines offers a way for fallible introspection to be used. It proposes that the method of independent testing be used on possibly false evidence as well as on true. If we have a false report—in our case a false introspective report—we can attempt to explain why it is false, using a theory which we then attempt to test independently. In this manner we can attempt to sift true from false introspective reports and, even more importantly, try to figure out what is going on in the mind even when the introspective report is inaccurate. That is, we can develop theories of the systematic inaccuracy and try to test them. Thus the motive for the move from introspectionist associationism—fear that the fallibility of introspective reports would make a scientific psychology impossible—is removed. What is still quite viable, as we can see from Popper's and Agassi's work, is non-associationist psychology which uses introspective reports as well as other evidence.

Just as Popper's approach removes the main methodological block to the views of the Külpe school, it also opens new paths for research into the psychology of learning. Whereas the Külpe school continued to identify learning with learning what is fixed and correct, Popper separated the two. This separation may open the way to a more fruitful consideration of the role of imagination in learning. And, as we have explained earlier, it raises a variety of interesting questions concerning when and how we change our theories or expectations in the light of evidence.

CURRENT VIEWS OF THE PROBLEM SITUATION IN THE METHODOLOGY OF SCIENCE

Philosophers, in contrast to psychologists, have not developed so unified a view of the current situation. In psychology there tends to be an up-to-date textbook version of the successes of the various schools, a version which exists even though psychologists may privately tend to dissent. In philosophy there is no such textbook version; each different school has its own views and its own version of the whole subject, and each school more openly views the other as misguided. The dominant views of methodology, as we have explained in Chapter 3, may be classified as inductive or conventionalist.

Each of these schools has central problems which are methodological analogues of the central problems of cognitive psychology; namely, how do we perceive? and how do we learn? For inductivists, these problems are how can we identify true observation statements? and how can we validly infer universal statements from observation statements? The latter problem has traditionally been the more important one because the former seemed to be more easily resolved. But the problem of correct inductive inferences presumes that we have a solution to the problem of how we can identify true observation statements. This identification problem has become severe under the impact of modern psychology.

According to modern psychology, especially that of the Gestalt and Würzburg schools, perception is influenced by predisposing attitudes and previous experience. But this means that scientific observation will be influenced by the theories of the observer—or, in the usual terminology, that observation is theory-impregnated. Thus proof of theory by observation may be illegitimately circular, and the inductivist approach collapses.

In conventionalism, the correlates of the psychological problems of perception and learning are somewhat different. First, conventionalism must demarcate between the theoretical framework, which is conventional, and the lower-level statements to be predicted, which must be true or false. We can make this demarcation if we regard observation statements as independent of theory, but we are contradicted by modern psychology. If we admit that observations are theory-impregnated, the demarcation is no longer clear. In consequence, there is a serious difficulty in distinguishing conventional from non-conventional elements.[3]

The second problem for conventionalists (analogous to the problem of learning) is the means of choosing frameworks which will enable us to steadily improve the predictive power of our theories. It is closer than it might seem to the problem of induction, since we need a theory of the choice of frameworks that will yield true predictions. Conventionalists have no easy answer to this question, for how do we know that the predictions a framework enables us to make correctly today will also hold true tomorrow?

Popper's methodology provides an alternative to both the inductivist and conventionalist schools. He accepts the realism of the inductivists but rejects their belief that we learn which theory is correct by inductive inference from observation. Let us now consider the impact of Popper's psychological ideas on the problems of the inductivist and conventionalist schools.

A REASSESSMENT OF THE PROBLEM SITUATION IN METHODOLOGY

We have sketched some of the standard problems in the philosophy of science and have suggested that they were made far more difficult by developments in modern psychology, especially in perception theory. Philosophers of science have, to a degree, recognized the importance of these developments, and have attempted to cope with them. The state of affairs in learning theory is somewhat different. Since the stimulus-response theories which generally have been regarded as the most successful in this area of study are variants of associationism, they have not posed a clear-cut challenge to philosophers of science. If

3. Joseph Agassi, *Science in Flux*, Chap. 5.

143

Popper's learning theory is taken seriously, however, additional deep problems are raised for standard philosophies of science: the two problems of learning—that of induction for inductivists, and of choosing (reliable) frameworks for conventionalists—are altered.

According to standard associationist views, we learn by making an inductive generalization when we observe discrete facts. If this generalization is properly made, it is justified. A recent modification of this theory separates the problems of the inductive genesis of theories from the inductive support of theories. The current view is that no matter how we initially reach a generalization, we do come to believe in it on the basis of repeated confirmations.

The approach of those holding this view (such as the "Bayesians") is to describe the psychological process of the strengthening of a belief by the addition of relevant evidence. It is hoped that this description will, at the same time, be able to refine the existing process of induction, or at least identify where faulty inductions could occur. Once we reject the Humean psychology underlying this approach, the program no longer seems to hold promise of being fruitful. According to the Würzburg theorists and Popper, our experiences are not the passive observation of "pure" atomic sense data; they are influenced and interpreted by means of our previous theories. Therefore, whatever the psychological process which strengthens or weakens our beliefs, it cannot be a purely inductive one, and the program of describing and refining the psychological process of inductive confirmation collapses.

An alternative is to reject the existence of an inductive psychological process of confirmation but still seek to form an inductive logic of choice of one theory over another. For example, Bühler accepted induction as a means of justification, even though he rejected it as a psychological process. However, it is known that any purely inductive inference is not valid by deductive standards; that is, the conclusion is not true in every possible world in which the premises are true. If we want to presume any type of inductive inference as a guide to choice and action, we are implicitly ruling out some possible events in the world. We must decide, then, whether to elevate the presumptions about the world to a 'logic' or to state our theories explicitly. It becomes evident that stating our theories explicitly is more desirable, for then we can use deductive logic to examine them critically, possibly to discover error in them, and to make improvements. Thus the search for an inductive logic of justification is ill-advised.

Popper's learning theory affects the conventionalist position in two ways. Poincaré was the first of many conventionalists to be concerned with the problem of how we use our imagination in extending scientific theories. Like Popper, he took a modified Kantian psychology as his starting point. His approach opened the way for serious consideration of the issue. Popper's view of the psychology of learning emphasizes the importance of the problem and the merits of Poincaré and his followers in attempting to deal with it.

Popper's theory also reveals a negative side to the conventionalist view. Conventionalists, like more traditional theorists, have regarded science as continuously developing, and this development is still identified with the fixation of a framework which may be extended but not overthrown. This stance has had a number of unsatisfactory consequences which, in the light of Popper's theory, cannot be avoided. We have already pointed out two of them: one is the need to make a sharp and stable division between theoretical science (which is conventional) and observation (which is realistic); the other is the need to justify the conventional framework by induction. In addition, an undesirable conservatism is introduced into scientific method. This conservatism is particularly vivid in Pierre

Duhem's work, but it is also a feature of all the conventionalist followers of Poincaré. They want existing scientific theory to be modified, but they do not want any of it to be *rejected*. In the light of Popper's psychology of learning, this sets an undesirable limit on the imagination.

A third approach to the philosophy of science has been made by Rudolf Carnap (1891–1970), who has attempted to be neutral in the conflict between different views of the psychology of learning and between realism and conventionalism. However, Popper's psychology makes it clear that this attempt at neutrality fails. Carnap initially proposed that some version of British associationism was correct. He acknowledged, particularly, the influence of Theodor Ziehen (1862–1950), who defended the British tradition from some of the contemporary attacks on it. Carnap clung to the associationist assumption that experience consists basically of discrete facts which are directly and correctly perceived, in spite of the later influence of Kurt Lewin (1890–1947). In order to have any knowledge beyond immediate perception, we need to relate these discrete facts in some orderly way. The problem of Carnap and his followers has been: how can we construct and justify our ordering principles?

Carnap's program can be interpreted in three different ways which are often intertwined and confused. First, it can be read inductively: we need to find true empirical laws which order the world. Secondly, it can be read in a conventionalist manner: the world can be ordered in many ways, but the aim of science is to find (at least) one *convenient* ordering. Thirdly, it can be read as a problem for logic: since the relation between facts should be described by logic, we need, for example, logical theories of 'necessity' and its use.

The key to solving the problem of induction, it has been thought, is to produce a logic which would indicate the possibility that a given ordering of discrete facts is correct.

The difficulty in justifying any ordering or theory which goes beyond existing facts has led some thinkers to shift to the second or third approach. On one hand, theories would not be regarded as realistic descriptions, and then an ordering would be justified as a useful or convenient device; on the other hand, perhaps one could reduce some of the needed ordering principles to principles of modal logic.

Criticisms of specific attempts to execute the Carnapian program may, of course, be made. For example, it has been claimed that there is no way to sensibly assign universal hypotheses a non-zero probability in a possibly infinite world. And it has been asserted that modal logic wrongly fuses logical and ontological questions; for example, there are different metaphysical conceptions of 'necessity'. It may be said as well that calling theories 'predictive devices' only disguises, and does not change, the fact that empirical claims are being made which go beyond previous observations. Though such criticisms may be sound, the Carnapian programs are misguided for a more fundamental reason.

That fundamental reason is that, in spite of the attempt at neutrality, they presume a false psychological theory; namely, that there exist pure, elementary sensations. These psychological limitations appear indirectly in discussions of the positivist research efforts, when the question of reducing theoretical to observational terms or of the independence of observation from theory is raised. But what goes unnoticed is that the work of Helmholtz, of the Würzburg school, and of the Gestalt psychologists has already thoroughly undermined the psychological presuppositions upon which the positivists base their program. We do not experience the world as a set of discrete and reliable facts, and, as Popper has argued, inductions from such facts do not exist.

As opposed to both the positivists and Popper, Michael

Polanyi has investigated the non-rational aspects of the choices made by scientists in the course of research. He has brilliantly revealed the importance of inarticulate or "tacit" knowledge in the process of problem solving; and he has described some of the important non-rational characteristics of the scientific community, such as some of the aspects of the apprenticeship of new researchers to older ones. In examining these factors, Polanyi has drawn on and developed ideas from Gestalt psychology. Similarly, Thomas Kuhn, in many respects a follower of Polanyi, has appealed to the perception theories of Gestalt psychology as a model for what happens during scientific revolutions, and he has similarly emphasized the non-rational characteristics of such transitions.

Polanyi has used his theory to argue against the possibility of useful rational rules of method. Kuhn has used his to argue against the value of rational criticism of a theory once it has become well-established in the scientific community. Popper, as would be expected, has strongly rejected these conclusions. We can see this disagreement in a clearer light when we recall the relation between Popper's psychology and the psychology of the Gestalt school.

The Gestalt psychologists used two concepts to describe the solving of problems, 'insight' and 'recentering', but, as we explained, they were unable to develop any fruitful theory of the nature of either one. Popper, on the other hand, provided a theory of the nature of a problem which causes restructuring and of the relation of the newly restructured knowledge to the previous state of knowledge. This theory indicated that logical relations could play an important role in that process. It would then seem to follow from Popper's psychology that the explicit debate over logical relations between theories and experiments could promote a perception of new and important problems and so stimulate the growth of science. In other words, if we take argument using logical deductions as the paradigm of rationality—as Popper does—then rational methods can promote the growth of science.

Thus the belief that Gestalt psychology supports a minimization of the role of reason in scientific research is incorrect: it is only that the Gestalt psychologists did not solve a problem—how Gestalt's change—which Popper has begun to solve. And Popper's efforts support the idea that rationality is of key importance in guiding research.

However, it is unfortunate that Popper went too far in the other direction, producing too rigid a model of the influence of reason on the choice of scientists. As we have seen, he has urged consensus on basic statements and has regarded them as, practically speaking, a stabile part of science. Popper did not, we should emphasize, make the error of the positivists and assert that any rational man, because of his rationality, would have to make the same choice of a given theory. He appealed to the promotion of the aims of science as a reason for adopting the rules of choice that he described. The rules, nonetheless, *do* fully determine choice. And this is both bad advice, and advice which smacks of the old mechanical ideal of rationality which Polanyi was trying to fight. It is also, as we have noted, in conflict with Popper's psychology.

The rules and techniques which can guide research, then, should be treated as rules which guide but do not fully determine choices. They should include techniques involving rational argument: the search for deductions of experimental results from theory, the search for counterexample, and the search for comparison with different world pictures. The challenge to the theory of scientific method is to produce and distinguish better and worse techniques and rules for individual decisions, to analyze and improve the social organization of science, and so on.

Since research is fundamentally a process of problem solving, these techniques (rational and non-rational) are essentially guides to the choice of problems, to the search for possible solutions, and to the evaluation of alternative possible solutions. As we noted earlier, Popper has recently put his theory of learning and of scientific method more into the framework of the theory of problem solving. Independently, there has been some development of the logic and psychology of problem solving. The challenge to the methodology of science is to find better guides to the problem solving process in science.

ACKNOWLEDGEMENTS

We wish to thank Joseph Agassi for encouraging us to expand what was originally an essay into this book, and for many stimulating discussions of Popper's philosophy and his own ideas. We are also grateful to Sir Karl Popper for discussions with one of us (Berkson) concerning his intellectual development and his critique of induction. Finally, we owe a special debt of gratitude to Hans Albert for his support for the earlier edition of this book, published in German translation by Hoffman & Campe Verlag. The present American edition contains some substantial changes in presentation, but not in content.

151

BIBLIOGRAPHY

Agassi, Joseph. "The Novelty of Popper's Philosophy of Science." *International Philosophical Quarterly* 8 (1968): 422–463.

————. *Science in Flux.* Edited by Robert S. Cohen and Marx W. Wartofsky. Boston Studies in the Philosophy of Science, vol. 28. Boston: D. Reidel Publishing Co., 1975.

Agassi, Joseph and Yehuda Fried. *Paranoia.* Boston Studies in the Philosophy of Science, vol. 50. Boston: D. Reidel Publishing Co., 1976.

Bacon, Francis. *Novum Organum.* Edited by Joseph Devey. Library of Universal Literature, pt. 1, vol. 22. New York: Collier, 1901.

Berkson, William. "Skeptical Rationalism." *Inquiry* 22: 281–320.

153

Bühler, Karl. *The Mental Development of the Child; A Summary of Modern Psychological Theory.* Translated from 5th German edition by Oscar Oeser. International Library of Psychology, Philosophy and Scientific Method. London: Paul, Trench, Trubner & Co., 1933.

Cohen, Robert S., and Marx W. Wartofsky, eds. *Methodological and Historical Essays in the Natural and Social Sciences.* Boston Studies in the Philosophy of Science, vol. 14. Boston: D. Reidel Publishing Co., 1974.

Flavell, John H. *The Developmental Psychology of Jean Piaget.* Princeton, N.J.: D. Van Nostrand Co., 1963.

Guthrie, Edwin Ray. *The Psychology of Learning.* rev. ed. Gloucester, Mass.: Peter Smith, 1960.

Hartmann, George Wilfried. *Gestalt Psychology: A Survey of Facts and Principles.* New York: Ronald Press Co., 1935.

Humphrey, George. *Thinking: An Introduction to Its Experimental Psychology.* London: Methuen & Co., 1951.

James R., "Conditioning is a Myth." *World Medicine* (18 May 1977): 25–28.

Kant, Immanuel. *Critique of Pure Reason.* Unabridged edition. Translated by Norman Kemp Smith. New York: St. Martin's Press, 1965.

Katz, David. *Gestalt Psychology: Its Nature and Significance.* Translated by Robert Tyson. New York: Ronald Press Co., 1950.

Locke, John. *An Essay Covering Human Understanding.* Edited by Peter H. Nidditch. Oxford: Clarendon Press, 1975.

Mandler, George, and Jean Matter Mandler. *Thinking: From Association to Gestalt.* New York: John Wiley, 1964.

Murphy, Gardner. *Historical Introduction to Modern Psychology.* New York: Harcourt Brace, 1949.

Newell, Allen, and Herbert A. Simon. *Human Problem Solving.* Englewood Cliffs, NJ.: Prentice-Hall, 1972.

Piaget, Jean. "Development and Learning." *Journal of Research in Science Teaching* 2: 184.

———. *Six Psychological Studies.* Edited by D. Elkind. Translated by Anita Tenzer. New York: Random House, 1967.

Poincaré, Henri. *Science and Hypothesis.* Translated by William John Greenstreet. New York: Dover Publications, 1952.

Popper, Karl. "Zur Methodenfrage der Denkpsychologie." Ph.D. diss., University of Vienna, 1928.

————. *Conjectures and Refutations.* London: Routledge & Kegan Paul, 1963.

————. *The Logic of Scientific Discovery.* 3d rev. ed. London: Hutchinson & Co., 1968.

————. *Objective Knowledge: An Evolutionary Approach.* Oxford: Clarendon Press, 1972.

————. *The Open Society and its Enemies.* 2 vol. 5th ed. Routledge & Kegan Paul, 1966.

————. *Unended Quest: An Intellectual Autobiography.* LaSalle, IL: Open Court Publishing Co., 1976.

Popper, Karl, and John C. Eccles. *The Self and Its Brain.* New York: Springer International, 1977.

Schilpp, Paul Arthur, ed. *The Philosophy of Karl Popper.* The Library of Living Philosophers, Vols. 14/1, 14/2. LaSalle, IL.: Open Court Publishing Co., 1974.

Selz, Otto. *Uber die Gesetze des geordneten Denkverlaufs.* Stuttgart: Spemann, 1913.

————. *Zur Psychologie des Produktiven Denkens und des Irrtums.* Bonn: Cohen, 1922.

Skinner, Burrhus, F. *Science and Human Behavior.* New York: Macmillan Co., 1953.

Tolman, Edward Chace. *Principles of Purposive Behavior.* n.p., 1957.

————. *Purposive Behavior in Animals and Men.* New York: The Century Co., 1932.

Wettersten, John. "Towards a Scientific Psychology: A Popperian Approach." Ph.D diss., Boston University, 1970.

————. "The Philosophy of Science and the History of Science: Separate Aspects vs. Separate Domains." *Philosophical Forum.* Forthcoming.

————. "Methods in Psychology: A Critical Case Study of Pavlov." *Philosophy of the Social Sciences* 4 (1974): 17–34.

————. "The Historiography of Scientific Psychology: A Critical Study." *Journal of the History of the Behavioural Sciences* (April 1975): 157–171.